License to Rape

LICENSE TO RAPE

Sexual Abuse of Wives

David Finkelhor
and Kersti Yllo

THE FREE PRESS
A Division of Macmillan, Inc.
NEW YORK

Library of Congress Cataloging-in-Publication Data

Finkelhor, David.
  License to rape.

  Bibliography: p.
  Includes index.
  1. Rape in marriage—United States. I. Yllo,
Kersti. II. Title.
[HV6561.F56   1987]   362.8′3   87-11935
ISBN 0-02-910401-7 (pbk.)

The Free Press
A Division of Macmillan, Inc.
866 Third Avenue, New York, N.Y. 10022

Collier Macmillan Canada, Inc.

Free Press Paperback Edition 1987

Printed in the United States of America

printing number

        3   4   5   6   7   8   9   10

This book is dedicated to the courageous
women who told us their stories

Contents

Acknowledgments

We have both been privileged to work in extremely congenial and nurturant intellectual environments. Depressing though the subject matter of family violence may at times be, it has attracted a group of scholars and professionals who are as generous, collegial, and stimulating as any we have ever met.

The Family Violence Research Program at the University of New Hampshire, where we both have our roots, is an unusually supportive environment. Staff and fellows of the program have given us a great deal of encouragement. They have enlivened the atmosphere with ideas from which we have both benefited. They have been friends and critics in the best sense of both words.

Murray Straus, the director of the program, has given a great deal to both of us. We hope that our work reflects some of his commitment to scholarship and honesty, and some of his belief in the applicability of social research to the improvement of the human condition. We are indebted and grateful to many other past and present members of the program. Ruth Miller, in helping to prepare the manuscript, probably spent more time involved in this project than any other person besides the authors. Her thoroughness and attention to detail and willingness to serve beyond the call of duty made the job incalculably easier and saved us from many disasters along the way. Her good nature helped us through some rough times. Sieglinde Fizz, with her remarkable administrative skill, kept the project on track at many critical moments.

Alice Downey made a crucial contribution toward the end of the project. Her careful editing left the manuscript much tighter and cleaner, and her energy kept the work moving along when it could have gotten bogged down. The final manuscript preparation was assisted by Heidi Gerhardt, Elaine Hashem, Kathy Hersh, Ann Noyes, and Nancy Shepardson. Diane Coleman and Valerie Hurst, graduate students in the program, helped with some of the interviewing. Members of the Family Violence Seminar, Larry Baron, Barbara Carson, Susan Herrick, Alan Lincoln, and, in particular, Debbie Kalmuss, Campbell Harvey, and Rich Sebastian, were valuable sources of information and gave us good constructive criticism of our ideas and writing. Lisa Someck helped to collect and analyze data on public attitudes.

Other colleagues in this field have also been generous with their help and criticism: Diana Russell, Jean Giles-Sims, Irene Freize, Julie Doron, Nick Groth, Nancy Shields, Gilbert Geis, Joanne Shulman, Martin Schwartz, Phyllis Gelman, Jodie Berger, and Richard Gelles.

Laura X of the National Clearinghouse on Marital Rape has supported our work enthusiastically from the beginning. Her careful work, voluminous archives, and critical feedback have helped us make this a better, more interesting book. Her research and that of her colleagues Jodie Berger, Sumaya Newland, Roxanne Alaniz, Shelly Barrios, Laurie Smelter, and Cathy Stephenson formed the basis of Appendix B. We are indebted to them for their diligent efforts. The Clearinghouse, an indispensable resource for anyone interested in doing research, education, or lobbying on the subject of marital rape, can be reached at 2325 Oak Street, Berkeley, California 94708; they have a firm policy of answering only those inquiries that contain self-addressed, stamped envelopes. We urge interested readers to become members and supporters of the Clearinghouse.

Agency staff made important, often very time-consuming contributions to the project, in some cases pirating time from otherwise overwhelming schedules to help. We would like to thank Jane Saunders, Priscilla Jenks, Bobby Goodnough, Debby Downs, Skee Frasee, Carol Paquette, Cindy Leerer, Kate McDonough, Lois Reckitt, and Ingrid Pilelo in particular.

Dean Raymond Erickson, attorneys Sherman McLaughlin, Louis Raveson, Joseph Bornstein, writer Mary Ellen Donovan, our agents, Barbara Grant, Fran Goldin, and our editors, Bobbi Mark and Rachel Christmas, also deserve appreciation. Kersti Yllo would also like to give special thanks to Rick Schwertner whose support and understanding have been invaluable throughout this project.

Our work has also been supported by the Eden Hall Farm Foundation, The Center for the Prevention and Control of Rape (a division of the National Institute for Mental Health), the National Center for Child Abuse and Neglect, and Wheaton College.

License to Rape

1
License to Rape

In most of the United States, a man cannot be prosecuted for raping his wife. Legally, he can sexually assault her in a dark alleyway. He can force her to submit with a knife at her throat. He can tie her up and have sex with her repeatedly, against her will. Whatever the degree of indignity, humiliation, or brutality he may impose on her, he will not wind up in jail for committing a rape.

He may, though, be prosecuted for some other crime that accompanied the rape: for hitting his wife, for threatening her with a weapon, or for kidnapping her. But the criminal charge will not be that he had sex with her against her will, without her consent.

The Illinois rape statute represents a typical case of how husbands are exempted from rape. A man commits a rape, it reads, when he has "sexual intercourse with a female, *not his wife*, by force and against her will."[1] All but twenty states incorporate similar exclusionary language in their laws. In some of the states, a husband retains immunity from prosecution from the moment his wife says "I do" until the ink dries on a divorce decree. By giving a man such immunity, the marriage license can indeed be called a "license to rape."

The "marital-rape exemption," as it is known, is not just an accidental loophole in the law. A doctrine with firm roots in our legal heritage that go back at least three hundred years, it is based on a theory of marriage and of sex within marriage that was first officially enunciated in the seventeenth century, by Matthew Hale, an influential English legal scholar. Hale wrote, "The husband cannot be guilty of rape committed by himself upon his lawful wife, for by their mutual matrimonial consent and contract, the wife hath given up herself in this kind unto her husband, which she cannot retract."[2]

Although this jurist was writing at a time when marriage was irrevocable and wives had no independent legal or economic rights, Hale's doctrine has endured. It has been incorporated into laws around the English-speaking world and reaffirmed again and again, as recently as 1977, by judges and lawyers writing about rape.[3] It has endured even though most of the other laws of that day concerning marriage—that a woman could not hold property, divorce, or live separately from her husband—have long since vanished.

Feminists have lately been taking aim at the marital-rape exemption and the theory that supports it. They have argued strongly that the notion that a husband cannot rape his wife is antiquated and should be stricken from the law.

For instance, Susan Brownmiller, whose 1975 book, *Against Our Will*, led the women's movement into the fight against rape, wrote, "A sexual assault is an invasion of bodily integrity and a violation of freedom and self-determination wherever it happens to take place, in or out of the marriage bed. . . . Compulsory sexual intercourse is not a husband's right in marriage, for such a 'right' gives lie to any concept of equality and human dignity."[4]

"Rape is rape," wrote Del Martin, one of the leaders of the movement to aid battered wives. "The identity of the rapist does not alter the fact of his act, nor lessen its traumatic effects on the victim.

The marital status of the parties involved should have no bearing on the definition of the crime of rape any more than it should on the crime of battery." She urged feminists not to "allow the men who control our legislatures to continue to exempt husbands from prosecution for rape when the women they rape are their wives."[5]

In the late 1970s, in response to such calls, feminists around the country began to mount legal and political efforts to remove the marital-rape exemption from the law books. Bills to criminalize rape in marriage were introduced in many state legislatures, and after intensive lobbying efforts, they were successful in California, Connecticut, New Jersey, Pennsylvania, as well as other states.

In four states—Florida, Massachusetts, New Jersey, and New York—court cases were also successful in challenging express or implied marital rape exemptions.[6] In what may set a trend for other states, these courts were highly critical of the Hale doctrine. They noted that historical circumstances had changed considerably since Hale's day, that rape statutes had gone through substantial recodifications, and that social conceptions of marriage and women's rights had been radically transformed. These courts all ruled that contemporary social and legal conditions did not support the existence of the Hale doctrine, that cohabiting husbands could indeed be prosecuted for rape, and, in the case of the New York court, that the marital rape exemption violated the equal protection clause of the U.S. constitution.

Although court decisions of this sort, legislative actions, and appeals from feminists have brought marital rape to public attention for what would appear to be the first time, the controversy about the "license to rape" is not new. The first wave of feminists, who swept America in the second half of the nineteenth century, also decried marital rape. Writers such as Elizabeth Cady Stanton detailed the many oppressive conditions that accompanied the condition of marriage,[7] and obligatory sex was one evil that she and others singled out for particular condemnation.

These feminists exclaimed that husbands "wasted women with

inordinate sexual desire"[8] and that a wife was "never free from brutal outrages, morning, noon and night, up almost to the very hour her baby was born and before she was again strong enough to move about."[9] But they did more than just focus on particular outrageous cases; they identified the law itself as contributing to women's sexual oppression. Pauline Wright Davis, for example, in an address to an 1871 meeting of the National Woman Suffrage Association, attacked the law that "makes obligatory the rendering of marital rights and compulsory maternity."[10] Elizabeth Cady Stanton wrote (rather rhetorically), "What father could rest at home by night, knowing that his lovely daughter was at the mercy of a strong man drunk with wine and passion and that, do what he might, he was backed up by law and public sentiment?"[11]

Nineteenth-century feminists had good cause to see marital rape as central to the struggle for women's autonomy. In the absence of safe, reliable, legal contraception or abortion, coerced sex and coerced childbearing were one and the same. If husbands could compel wives to have sex, they could compel them to have babies—an activity that in those days could involve a substantial risk to life. As Linda Gordon writes: "The right of the wife unilaterally to refuse her husband: this is at the heart of voluntary motherhood. It was a key substantive demand in the mid-nineteenth century when both law and practice made sexual submission to her husband a woman's duty. A woman's right to refuse is clearly the fundamental condition of birth control and of her independence and personal integrity."[12]

The nineteenth-century feminists did win many important changes in the legal foundations of marriage, but laws clearly protecting women from sexual coercion by their husbands were not among these. Their fight for voluntary motherhood was eventually overshadowed by the twentieth-century struggle, led by Margaret Sanger, for the right to obtain and distribute effective contraception. Women became convinced that the most immediate liberation from the burdens of enforced childbearing could come through birth control. During the period of the struggle for contraception and abortion rights, the issue of forced sex became a subordinate concern. This in part had to do with the waning of a militant feminist movement that would radically criticize marriage and its economic and legal foundations. It was not until the second wave of American feminism, in the late 1960s, and the resurgence of criticism of the nuclear family, that the issue of forced sex in marriage again became the subject of public debate.

Unfortunately, the current controversy has centered almost entirely on the legal aspects of marital rape. While the courts and legislatures have received attention, the victims themselves have been virtually ignored. The reality of the crime has been left to people's imaginations, which tend to conjure up images to suit their own prejudices. Little effort has been made to gather or present social-scientific information on the subject. In fact, the phenomenon is so remote from some people's reality that they find it hard to imagine that it exists at all.

The lack of public awareness about the reality of marital rape can be ascribed largely to the secrecy surrounding the problem, a secrecy maintained by most parties to the problem—victims, abusers, and the public at large. Victims are ashamed. Abusers help to keep them quiet and intimidated through threats, emotional blackmail, and a kind of "brainwashing" that makes the victims feel that they are to blame. The rest of us feel awkward, uncomfortable, and helpless to do anything, so we choose not to ask and not to hear.

Many women who have been sexually assaulted by their husbands do not see themselves as having been raped. They tend to view the assault as part of a marital conflict for which they are to blame, wondering if their own inadequacies as wives and partners are at the root of the problem and believing their own sexual problems provoke their husbands. That their husbands are violent is taken by many to be a judgment on themselves: a judgment that they could not maintain a normal marriage or please their partners enough. A marital rape is part of a personal shame that they do not want others to know.

But, of course, the rest of us do not make it easy for women who have been sexually assaulted to tell anyone about their situation. Marital rape as a social problem is rarely discussed in public circles. Moreover, by formally exempting such behavior from criminal prosecution, society, in effect, states that it is not a matter of concern to our institutions. Public officials do not give victims any reason to believe they can expect help. People in the helping professions do not receive training that might lead them to inquire about this kind of abuse. Stories about victims of such crimes are only rarely included on television or in the newspapers, where women might see them and take note that they are not alone. Even the social-science literature has been devoid of information on the subject. Out of thirty-one marriage and family textbooks published in the 1970s, we found only one that mentioned marital rape or anything related.

When we began our research in 1979, there was little more than speculation about the nature and scope of marital rape—whether it was a crime that affected a great many women or just a few; whether it was violent and frightening to the victim; whether women were in fact traumatized by it, as Del Martin suggested.

As sociologists working in the area of family violence, we decided to conduct research to answer these questions and to extend our knowledge on this overlooked aspect of marriage. The first part of our research—a survey of 323 Boston-area women undertaken in 1980 and 1981—investigated prevalence and demographics: how widespread marital rape is and whether it occurs more often to women of certain educational or economic backgrounds than to others. (For more information on the design of the survey, see Appendix A.)

Our survey showed disturbingly high rates of sexual assault by husbands. *Ten percent of the married or previously married women in our sample said that their husbands had "used physical force or threat to try to have sex with them.*"[13] We do not know whether *all* these assaults meet the precise legal definition of rape or attempted rape. For example, we do not know how many of the reported sexual assaults involved intercourse and how many involved other sexual acts. Nonetheless, 10 percent of the 323 Boston-area married women did report an experience that qualifies as a sexual assault by a husband since it included the use of physical force or threat of physical force.

Another revealing finding of our survey was that sexual assault by husbands was among the most common kinds of sexual assault. When people think of rape, they tend to think of its being committed by someone unknown to the victim, yet this is not consistent with reality. Rape by a stranger is the variety that is most likely to be reported to police, yet 10 percent of the women in our study had been sexually assaulted by their husbands, whereas only 3 percent had been similarly assaulted by a stranger (see Table A-1 in Appendix A). In addition, rape by a date was reported by 10 percent of the women. Clearly, sexual assaults by intimates, including husbands, are by far the most common type of rape. Thus rape by husbands appears to be one of the forms of sexual coercion that a woman is most likely to experience in her lifetime.

Diana Russell's 1978 survey of sexual-assault experiences of women in San Francisco, California, also establishes that marital rape occurs to millions of married women each year.[14] She and her staff interviewed over nine hundred women, eighteen or older, who had been scientifically selected as representative of all the women living in that city. The women were questioned about sexual assaults involving strangers, dates, family members, and also husbands.

Russell found that 12 percent of the married women had had an experience that would qualify under the legal definition of rape in California: "forced intercourse or intercourse obtained by physical threat or intercourse completed when the woman was drugged, unconscious, asleep or otherwise totally helpless and unable to consent." Another 2 percent reported that they had been forced to engage in some other form of sexual activity, such as oral or anal sex. Thus a total of 14 percent of the wives had been sexually assaulted in some manner by their husbands.[15] As we did, Russell found marital rape to be among the most common kinds of sexual assault: more than twice as many women in her study had been raped by a husband as by a stranger.[16]

Although precautions were taken to promote candor in both studies, it is very likely that our count and Russell's count of sexual-assault experiences in marriage are on the low side. When one is dealing with such a sensitive subject, it is inevitable that some women would not feel comfortable enough to reveal what had happened to them. Moreover, some women may have neglected to mention some sexual assaults they had experienced in previous marriages. In other words, although between 10 and 14 percent of the married women surveyed acknowledged a sexual assault by a husband, the real incidence is probably even higher.

Are there any particular groups of women who appear to report unusually numerous incidents of forced sex? In our survey, we estimated the rates of forced sex for women by various social characteristics, such as education, income, and marital status, and found that some women do seem to be more vulnerable than others (see Tables A-1 to A-10 of Appendix A).

First, separated and divorced women reported especially numerous incidents of forced sex. One in every four divorced or separated women said her husband had used force or threats to try to have sex with her. It is not surprising that the rate would be higher for these women. In some cases marital rape is clearly one of the reasons that women leave marriages. In others, rape is the husband's response to his wife's decision to separate for other reasons.

Our survey also shows a tendency for marital-rape victims to come from lower social-class backgrounds, particularly among women who are still living with their partners. In that group, women who did not finish high school reported four times more marital rape than those who did. We also found that women

8

whose current family incomes were under ten thousand dollars had more marital-rape experiences. This also is not surprising, since these women would be less financially capable of leaving their partners.

The implication of these findings must be carefully emphasized. Though our survey shows marital rape to be somewhat related to social class, it also shows marital rape to be democratically distributed. It certainly cannot be argued, on the basis of what we found, that marital rape is *limited* to lower social classes. In fact, our statistics show that one out of fourteen women with graduate work or a graduate degree has been forced to have sex by her husband.

Our survey also provided a look into the relationship of marital rape to other characteristics of the victim and assaulter, such as race, ethnicity, and religion of victim and assaulter. Among the small number of black women surveyed, we found no significantly higher rate of marital rape than among white women. The survey does show that the rates for Protestants and those reporting no religion at all were higher than those for Catholics or Jews. It also shows women under thirty and over fifty reporting more forced sex. Finally, women who were sexually victimized as children were almost three times more likely to be sexually victimized again by a husband. Although this finding has been confirmed by other researchers, the reason victims of child sexual abuse may be at higher risk for marital rape is not clearly understood. We can speculate that women who are trying to escape from abuse in their family of origin are less discriminating about the partners they choose and are easy prey to men looking for someone to dominate.

But statistics can tell only a small part of the marital-rape story. The second phase of our study involved in-depth interviews, one to two and a half hours in length, with victims of marital rape. Here we learned more details about the experience—how the victim perceives the assault at the hands of her spouse and how she is affected by it. We also learned about the men who commit mar-

9

ital rape: who they are and what techniques they use to force themselves upon their wives.

Most of the women who shared their experiences with us were clients of various family-planning agencies in the New England area. Such agencies, which see a large number of women from diverse backgrounds, are comfortable settings for research of this sort. Since visits there already concern sexual matters, asking about coercive sex is not out of context. Also, many women have strong allegiances to their family-planning agencies, which they know to be staffed by sensitive and concerned women to whom they can turn for advice about often difficult and emotional subjects like contraception and abortion. Under the system we worked out, when women came to the agency they were asked whether any current or previous partner had ever used force or threatened force to try to have sex with them. If they answered yes, they were invited to participate in an interview. Each woman was paid ten dollars for her time and any cost incurred, such as that of a babysitter or transportation. We felt that this sum provided some compensation, but was not so great as to coax a reluctant individual into participating.

Although the family-planning agencies were our main source of interviews, a number of women came from other places. Some volunteered after hearing one of us speak; a small group came from battered-women's shelters; and a few responded to an ad we placed in *Ms*. magazine. (For more details on the sample, see Appendix A.)

Many people find it hard to imagine that women would willingly talk to researchers about so intimate and sensitive a subject as marital rape, but we were not surprised. After conducting research for several years on such highly sensitive subjects as child abuse, sexual abuse, and wife abuse, we have come to realize that a great many people welcome a researcher's inquiry into their private matters. Far from recoiling when asked to talk about such subjects, many people, we have found, say that talking gives them satisfaction and relief. For some women our study was a way to open up about something they had wanted to talk about for a long time. As one woman who had been afraid to mention the subject to anyone else before said to us, "I knew you would understand about it. After all, it's your job. I knew you had heard about these things before." Women believed that a researcher would give them a sympathetic hearing, without being shocked or judgmental.

Sometimes, the mere fact that a study was being conducted about this subject came as a revelation to a marital-rape victim. "I knew," said one, "that if you were doing a study on this subject, I couldn't be the only one it had happened to." For her, and for other women, the study was a chance to feel less alone. These women readily gravitated to the study as a way of gaining some consolation about their experience.

There was another theme that ran through the interviews. Many of the women came to talk about their sexual assaults as a way of overcoming the suffering and isolation and embarrassment that the experience had caused them. Talking about it was a way of putting it behind them. They wanted to tell the story of how they had finally escaped from the impossible marriage, how they had finally overcome timidity and fear and learned to act in their own behalf. The accounts of some of these women had an almost inspirational quality.

Finally, the most touching testimonials came from women who felt strongly that they could help other women by telling their stories. In a letter to us volunteering to be interviewed, a woman wrote, "If one word or one sentence I would say to you could keep one young woman from making the same mistake I did, give one woman the courage to leave such a marriage, or open one man's eyes to what he was doing and why, it would be worth the pain of opening healed wounds."

Ultimately, we interviewed fifty women, and the stories they shared with us—with names and identifying details changed—constitute the core of this book. Our goal in conducting the research and writing this book is to provide genuine information about marital rape and make it available to the public at large, especially to all those concerned with the problem. As part of this effort, one of our most important objectives is to present the testimony of marital-rape victims themselves. We believe the stories of women who have been victims of marital rape need to be told, that marital rape cannot be adequately understood or addressed without a full picture of what they have experienced. The fact that marital rape is legal in most states does not lessen the violation these women endured. Marital rape exists. We need to understand it in order to end it.

2
The Myth and Reality of Marital Rape

For most people, forced sex in marriage has little to do with what they would call "real" rape. When they think of "real" rape, they think of a stranger, a weapon, an attack, a threat to a woman's life. Forced marital sex, on the other hand, conjures up an unpleasant, but not particularly serious, marital squabble.

This attitude toward marital rape as a rather innocuous event was vividly illustrated when we solicited fictitious descriptions of marital rape from over four hundred university students. Here are some of the typical replies:

> He wants to. She doesn't. He says, "That's tough, I'm going to anyway," and he does.

> Husband and wife are newly separated. He comes for a short visit and forces her to make love because he really does love her and misses her.

> The wife was unwilling to have sex and he forced himself on her.

These images of marital rape constitute what we call the "sanitary stereotype"—marital rape depicted as a petty conflict. People do not regard it as very serious because in their minds the action itself is not very dramatic. To most, it is a disagreement over sex that the husband wins. Their images are very bland: little graphic violence, little pain, little suffering. The coercion involved is abstract; people use neutral phrases like "he forced her" or "he makes her" to describe the rape.

These accounts contrast noticeably with the graphic descriptions one usually gets for scenarios of rape by a stranger. In these descriptions, a woman is often pictured walking home late at night when a man grabs her, drags her into an alley, pulls out a knife, and rapes her. The stereotype gives plenty of fodder for fear and outrage. One would hardly expect to hear a description of stranger rape that went: "They met on the street. He wanted to. She didn't." Even "He accosted her on the street and he forced himself on her" would be an unusually cursory description of rape by a stranger. But these were just the kind of flat accounts many of our respondents gave in picturing marital rape.

The sanitary stereotype that people conjure up when asked about marital rape is a product of ignorance and misinformation. Relatively few personal stories about raped wives have appeared on film or television, or even in popular literature. Most that have make marital rape appear almost romantic.

Perhaps the most familiar movie imagery of marital rape comes from *Gone with the Wind*. There, a "healthily sexual" man, Rhett Butler (Clark Gable), overcomes the resistance of proper and frightened Scarlett O'Hara (Vivian Leigh), and carries her struggling upstairs to an outcome left to the viewer's imagination. The next scene shows Scarlett the morning after, preening and glowing with barely repressed exhilaration and love. *Gone with the Wind* presents a most dangerous image of marital rape, for it powerfully advertises the idea that women secretly wish to be overpowered and raped, and that, in fact, rape may be a good way to reconcile a marriage.

Coal Miner's Daughter offers a more current version of marital rape. There, young Loretta (Sissy Spacek) is carried off into marriage by a dashing—and obviously experienced—Mooney (Tommy Lee Jones). She knows little of what to expect from sex. As he roughly climbs on top of her, she senses that he is about to do something violent and awful. She tries to struggle and push him away, but he is so big that he overpowers her, and she is left frightened and sobbing.

Media images such as these mislead in their portrayals of marital rape as primarily about sex. Typically, the man is depicted as having a healthy, if a bit overzealous, sexual appetite, while the woman is seen as being repressed or squeamish. But even when the man is portrayed as a brute and his wife as a "healthily sexual" woman, the problem triggering the rape is still presumed to be a conflict over sex. We may disapprove of his methods, but we cannot help approving of his ends: conjugal relations.

Moreover, such media images present marital rape as a kind of trivial event, like an argument over what restaurant to go to. There is love underneath, even if passions get unruly, and it would be a travesty of the highest order if Rhett Butler or Mooney ended up facing a five-year jail term for their excess of passion. No wonder people are startled by the idea of criminalizing marital rape.

Fortunately, another version of marital rape, a more realistic and alarming one, is bit by bit coming to supplant the sanitary renditions produced by Hollywood and the popular culture. As laws change across the country, stories of marital rapes are finding their way onto police blotters and sometimes into the newspapers. Through such stories, the myths of marital rape are being replaced with the reality of violation and brutality.

Sarasota, Florida, *Herald Tribune*—August 28, 1981

A 23-year-old Bradenton man has been formally charged by the state attorney's office with raping his wife, who is a paraplegic.

The man, who is not being named to protect the identity of his wife, was arrested for sexual battery after a neighbor in the couple's apartment complex on 26th Street West called police to report screams coming from a nearby apartment.

When the deputy arrived, the victim reported that she had been beaten a few days earlier and claimed she had lost several teeth. The deputy said she could see bruises on the woman's face.

The wife signed an affidavit alleging that her husband had committed anal and oral intercourse on her over a period of three days. The woman is reportedly paralyzed from her ribs to her toes.

State Attorney James A. Gardner said his office considered this case just as they do other rape cases. He said he was not aware of any other cases in this circuit in which a husband had been charged with raping his wife while they were still living together.

Vista, California, *Vista Press*—September 20, 1981

A La Costa man has pleaded guilty to raping his wife, in what may be a North County first under a fairly new state law making spousal rape a crime.

Daniel Herwich, 39, pleaded guilty Wednesday before Superior Court Judge Charles Froehlich. The case was set to begin Monday with jury selection.

His former wife, Suzanne, 39, charged that he forced her car off the road, threatened to kill her and twice choked her into unconsciousness. She was later treated for extensive bruises all over her body and was X-rayed for a possible broken arm.

In a July preliminary hearing, Mrs. Herwich testified that she filed divorce papers in March and moved from the La Costa Avenue home to Los Angeles. She did not give Herwich her new address or telephone number, she said.

On April 18, he showed up at the hairdressing salon where she worked, and begged her to have a date with him. She said she felt sorry for him and agreed to have brunch with him on April 26.

That day she drove to his home, picked him up and they ate at a nearby deli. They talked about the divorce and she said she was not coming back to him.

Mrs. Herwich said she dropped off her husband at home, then joined friends for a day of golf in San Marcos. When she left them at about 8 p.m., her route to the freeway took her past Herwich's house.

She noticed a car's headlights approach rapidly from the rear, then pull alongside her car. Herwich was inside, she said, and he began cutting in front of her, forcing her to a stop.

When he told her to return home with him, she complied because she believed his car would outrun hers if she tried to speed away, Mrs. Herwich testified.

At the house, Herwich allegedly grabbed her by the arm, pushed her inside and said she was going to die. He shoved her into the family room, against a wall bar, she said, and choked her twice.

He nearly let her go then, threatening to kill her "next time." But before she got through the door he pulled her back inside, Mrs. Herwich continued.

She said he ripped open the zipper on her jeans and pulled them off, along with her underpants. He dragged her back to the family room, she said, tore her blouse and bra, and raped her.

Afterwards, he got up and apologized, and Mrs. Herwich pulled on her clothes and hurried away. She drove several blocks to a gas station telephone and called her golfing friends.

They picked her up, brought her to their home, then took her to Scripp's Hospital where she reported the rape to police.

These are hardly marital squabbles or minor events in the lives of the victims. And though newspapers tend to report more extreme cases, the crimes perpetrated on the women we interviewed rival these.

To the women we talked to in the course of our study, marital rapes were frightening and brutal events that usually occurred in the context of an exploitative and destructive relationship. This sexual abuse was only peripherally about sex. More often it was about humiliation, degradation, anger, and resentment. Women were left, if not physically disabled, then psychologically traumatized for a long time.

- one was jumped in the dark by her husband and raped in the anus while slumped over a woodpile;
- one had a six-centimeter gash ripped in her vagina by a husband who was trying to "pull her vagina out";
- one was gang-raped by her husband and a friend after they surprised her alone in a vacant apartment;
- one was raped at knifepoint by her estranged partner;
- one was forced to have sex the day after returning from gynecological surgery, causing her to hemorrhage and obliging her to return to the hospital;
- one was forced to have sex with her estranged husband in order to see her baby, whom he had kidnapped.

The list could go on. Our interviewees were not chosen because their assaults were especially severe. They were, for the most part, women at local family-planning agencies and battered-women's shelters who admitted, when asked, that their husbands had forced them to have sex. The indignities they suffered are not unusual; they are the kind of marital rapes that show up when someone asks women to talk about the issue.

The sanitized image of marital rape routinely omits the component of terror. Many of the women we talked to told of marriages in which they had been beaten for years; of men who would turn on them unexpectedly at the slightest provocation; of homes they were afraid to leave. The quality of their lives was in some ways like a Grimm fairy tale: they lived with ogres whose violence, anger, and unpredictability kept them constantly in fear of where and when the next blow would come.

Shirley, a thirty-two-year-old woman with three children, was working on the staff of a battered-women's shelter. She was referred to us by the other staff members.

Shirley had met her husband while he was in the military, and married him after knowing him for only a few months. He came from an affluent Southern family, his father was a doctor, and he had received a scholarship to a prestigious university.

She liked him at first because he was such a "perfect gentleman," the kind who opened doors, took her coat, and hung it up. He could be caring and playful, and they had had many good times together. But he had a Dr.-Jekyll-and-Mr.-Hyde quality. At times of stress, pressure would build up in him. His eyes would turn red, and he would explode. "It was like he turned into a different person," she said. She could sense it coming on, but the change itself might occur in seconds, with no connection to any alcohol or drug abuse.

At first his outbursts only occurred at work. (He had a steady job as a carpenter.) But then they began to involve her. For example, during his episodes he would force her to sit in a chair for hours on end while he watched her. If she looked at the clock, she got hit. If she said something he did not like, she got slapped or thrown to the floor.

One of these ordeals occurred when she was pregnant. He yanked her out of a chair and rammed her head into a cabinet. The concussion she sustained left her disoriented for five days, and she had a miscarriage. He abused their daughter, too. He had something against women, she felt, perhaps connected to his strong resentment of his mother.

19

In many ways, Shirley was a classic battered woman. Frequently black and blue, she was terrified of her husband's temper. And as a woman with little education and a number of children, she believed she could not survive without him. One time he spent all his earnings on his motorcycle and gave her five dollars for the week's groceries. Stunned, she spilled some milk on the floor as she protested that she could never feed the family on that small amount. He pushed her to the floor, poured the rest of the milk over her, and mopped it up with her hair and her clothes. But she never got angry with him, she reported: "Anger was not a word allowed in my vocabulary."

Others apparently knew about the abuse but were of no help, or worse. Her mother had seen him try to kill her. Once Shirley sought refuge in her mother's house, but he came after her with a knife, saying, "If I can't have her, no one can." After that, the mother refused to let Shirley stay with her.

An extremely religious person and a member of a fundamentalist church, Shirley told her pastor many times about the beatings; he counseled her to forgive her husband.

In spite of the violence, Shirley reported that for the most part their sexual relationship was very good. Even after all the pain he caused her, she still looks back favorably on the sex. She thinks that it may have been the only thing that kept the relationship going at times. One could hardly characterize his sexual behavior as conventional, however. He apparently engaged in peeping on neighbors at different times in their marriage; once, shortly after she gave birth, thirteen neighbors appeared at her door to ask her to keep him from doing so. He also had many affairs with other women. She knows of three whom he got pregnant—and who came to her about it. Her pastor told her to forgive him for this, too.

The sex was good, yet he would also rape her. These rapes generally occurred during his tantrums, in the midst or at the end of beatings. She had a hard time saying exactly how frequent they were.

One particularly savage sexual assault occurred after they had

had an argument and she had gone into the shower to try to put some distance between them. He came into the bathroom and kept ripping back the curtain. She slapped him, something she had never done before (and never did again: "That taught me"). He started socking her in the stomach, until she vomited. Then he forced her to have sex. Distraught, she thought she might finally get some assistance from her pastor and quickly dialed his number. Before she could tell him what had happened, however, her husband picked up the phone on another extension and shouted, "I just raped my wife! What are you going to do about it, pastor?"

She was finally able to get out of the marriage, but not unscathed. An acquaintance had given her the name of a shelter, and, at wit's end one day, she called up and demanded to be taken, even though the shelter had no room. While she was staying there, her husband found out its location and arrived at the door in a fury. She was frightened to death, she remembers, so immobilized that it was all she could do to crawl upstairs to safety on her hands and knees, "like a whipped dog with my tail between my legs." The staff at the shelter called the police, who came and removed her husband.

After rest and recuperation at a convent, she got a divorce and thought she was in the clear. But her husband was not done with her. One night he showed up at her apartment, and since he demanded to talk about the kids, she let him in. They talked; he put on his hat and coat as if to go. She had to tend to another member of her household, and when she was finished she assumed he had left. But when she had undressed and got into bed, to her horror she discovered that he had hidden in her bedroom closet. He got into bed with her and forced her to do something he knew she hated—oral sex. "Eat it," he commanded her. "Eat it or I'm gonna stick it up your ass." "This is what you deserve," he told her. "Then he got up and left as if nothing had happened," she said.

"The whole thing was just 'I have control, I have force over you, and I'll make you do what I damn well please.' . . . I thought I had divorced this guy to get out of this situation and here I still am at

21

the edge of it. It took a long time for me to pull myself together."
But with the help of the shelter, she is pressing charges.

Many marital-rape victims are, like Shirley, battered wives, and entrapment and terror are part and parcel of their lives. Her story illustrates many of the elements of the classic battering situation: the husband becomes increasingly brutal; his outbursts are capricious and unpredictable; he comes to dominate her life and makes threats to deter her from leaving or acting independently.

About half of the women in our sample of marital-rape victims were battered. Not all were as terrorized and brutalized as Shirley, but all had experienced repeated physical attacks, often connected to drunkenness. For the remainder of this chapter we will talk primarily about the rape experiences of these battered wives, and what their histories have in common. They were the most brutalized and terrorized of the marital-rape victims, and their stories are the ones that clash most starkly with the sanitary stereotype of marital rape. (There was also a large group of women in our sample who were not battered wives. Since their experiences were somewhat different, they deserve separate treatment; we will discuss them in the next chapter.)

Battered women are at especially high risk of sexual assault. Studies of battered women regularly show that anywhere from a third to a half of them are victims of marital sexual assault.[1] Clearly, a husband who is capable of punching and slapping his wife repeatedly is also capable of using force to make his wife have sex with him. In fact, what is surprising is that some batterers who could easily coerce their wives into sex are for some reason inhibited from doing so.

We noted certain common features in the marital rapes that occurred in battering relationships. First, the sexual violence in these relationships was another aspect of the general abuse. These men hit their wives, belittled them, called them names,

22

took their money, and, as another way of humiliating and degrading them, resorted to sexual violence.

Often the sexual abuse was a continuation of the beatings. Husbands would find a pretext and start to attack. Beatings might last for an hour, or for a day. At some point, usually toward the end of the beating, the husband would either strip his wife or force her to disrobe and then have intercourse. Forty percent of the women we interviewed described one of these beating-plus-rape combinations.

When rapes followed physical assaults, two different patterns occurred. Sometimes, the hitting and the punching would continue throughout the sex, and the sex itself would be full of violence. In other cases, the men would act as though they were finished with the beating and wanted to make up with a little sex. The women, exhausted and in pain from the beating and hardly feeling close to their husbands, would not want to be touched. In these cases, the husbands would roughly push themselves on their exhausted partners or threaten them with more violence unless they complied.

Marital-rape incidents were not isolated episodes in these marriages. In the sanitary stereotype, a marital rape might be a once-in-a-relationship occurrence, something quite rare that happens under unusual circumstances. Exactly 50 percent of the women in our study said they had been sexually assaulted twenty times or more. (In other studies the percentage of repeatedly raped victims runs from 59 percent to 87 percent.[2]) And for the majority of the women we talked to, rape was a repeated occurrence. For some, assaults were so common they could not remember how often. "It happened half of the time we had sex during those three years," said one woman typical of this group. For most marital-rape victims, rape is a chronic and constant threat, not an isolated problem. The battered women, of course, were the most vulnerable of all to such repeated sexual abuse. Twice as many battered women suffered from chronic rapes (twenty times or more) as the other raped women. In addition to being punching bags, the battered women were also, as one woman put it, "masturbating machines."

One cannot say that the marital rapes of these battered women occurred because of a conflict over sex. Rather, the rapes they suffered were an extension of the other violence. Many times the incidents occurred suddenly, without having anything lead up to them. One woman's husband dragged her off into the bedroom while they were entertaining guests. Another grabbed and raped her when she was on the way to the bathroom. These assaults had much of the same unprovoked character as the battering assaults, which also could occur over nothing more serious than her forgetting to buy his cigarettes or wanting to watch a different television show. The attacks seemed like capricious expressions of anger and resentment. Though they were sexual acts, they were not sparked by sexual disagreements.

What illustrated the basically nonsexual motivation of the rapes we studied is, ironically, that many of the battered wives said that they enjoyed having sex with their husbands when they were approached with genuine desire and affection. But instead of wooing their wives to bed, the husbands would beat them up and then demand sex, or jump them roughly with no preliminaries whatsoever. Such men were not using force because their wives were reluctant to comply. Rather, they were using force because they wanted to frighten, humiliate, punish, and degrade.

This theme of sex as punishment and retaliation is well conveyed in the account of Shirley, who was completely dominated and terrorized by her husband. He put her through the most humiliating rituals of subservience and obedience. The two marital rapes she described in detail were both clear examples of retaliation and revenge. In one case rape was her punishment for striking back at him; he even crowed about his accomplishment over the phone to the pastor. In the other case—forcing her to fellate him—he was punishing her for daring to divorce him.

Shirley's last rape was typical of the quarter of the women in our sample who said they had been assaulted even after their separation or divorce. Many, like Shirley, had believed they were finally safe and out of the clutches of their husbands. Usually the husband came to the woman's house in the evening or late at night, under the pretext of retrieving some clothes or wanting to talk about the kids or the custody arrangement. Often he had been drinking. At some point in the conversation, he would become belligerent and begin to demand his "rights." "You're still my wife and I can do what I want with you," one shouted.

A wife's leaving or threatening to leave her marriage frequently provokes a marital rape. Irene Frieze, in fact, found that among the group of battered women she studied, leaving or threatening to leave was the factor that was most often associated with a sexual assault.[3] In our study, over two-thirds of the women in our sample were raped in the waning days of a relationship, either after previous separations or when they were making plans to get out.

Among the eighty-seven marital-rape victims in Diana Russell's study, ten were raped after they were separated. For six of the women it was the first time their husbands raped them. Three women were raped by their ex-husbands after they were divorced. Thus, 15 percent of the women (or one in seven) were raped after their marriages were terminated.[4]

The rapists who attacked toward the end of relationships or after separations obviously had retaliatory motives. These husbands, furious that their wives had gathered up the courage to leave, used the assault as a way to express their anger and punish their wives. Shirley's husband made that objective clear.

Some of the men seemed devastated at the thought of losing their wives and at seeing their connection and control disappearing. What they could not have willingly, they attempted to win back through a brute display of sexual power. "You know you're gonna like it. You liked it for that long. You're gonna like it again," one man screamed as he raped his wife, having learned she would not return to him.

Marital rapes are also quite common at the end of relationships because husbands feel they have nothing more to lose. One man, who knew his deteriorating marriage was headed for a break-up, tackled his wife and forced her to have anal intercourse—something he had always wanted but she had prevented in the course of the relationship. She commented, "I guess he realized that the relationship was over and he might as well have his way before we split up; sort of, I'll do it to you because it doesn't matter anymore!"

Twenty-one-year-old Katherine was interviewed at a battered-women's shelter where she had been living with her two-year-old son. She had recently escaped, for the second time, from her violent husband of almost three years.

Katherine remembered her family as a very nice one. Her parents did a great deal for her and her two siblings. There was never any arguing between them, and only once can she remember being spanked. Her father was a painter and a carpenter, while her mother took care of the family.

She met her future husband at a McDonald's, and they went together for a year before she got pregnant. He had just joined the army, but within two months he was out with a dishonorable discharge, and they married.

Their marriage was good at first but deteriorated suddenly and quickly. He was drinking a lot, and in the fifth month of her pregnancy he had an affair with another woman. Then, in the eighth month of her pregnancy, his violence came to the surface.

One night when he had returned home drunk, Katherine complained to him about his running around with other women. First he picked up a broom and hit her with it. Then he pulled out a knife and warned her, "I'm gonna cut your throat." Terrified, she ran into the bathroom and locked the door. He told her to open it or he would cut her guts out; when she didn't, he began to kick down the door.

This fracas awakened a friend of his who was staying in the apartment, and he came into the room to try to subdue the husband. While her husband was distracted, Katherine escaped from the bathroom and ran outside to hide in the bushes, but not before her husband had thrown a big tackle box at her. She was waiting in the bushes when the police and rescue squad arrived, to find that her husband had stabbed his friend four times—three times in the leg and once in the lung. The friend was rushed to the hospital and survived. The husband, convicted of assault, spent three months in jail before he was freed on a work-release program.

Although this was the peak of his violent behavior, there was also a more routine kind of abuse that he directed at her. He was hitting her every day. He was going out, leaving her behind, and getting drunk. Out of a job, he was letting her earn their living in a shoe store or at a deli, while he hung around the house. He was running around with other women. And he used a novel method to get her to quit smoking: he punched her in the mouth whenever she lit a cigarette.

One night he knocked her out completely with a punch in the mouth. Another time he threw a knife at her. That same evening, in front of his parents, he threw her to the ground and kicked her in the head. He burned her with a cigarette. He locked her in their shed for an evening. His mother warned her to leave: "He's gonna kill you." Then, when she did so, the mother begged her to go back to him, because he was so distraught she thought he would commit suicide.

In the context of such abuse, it is no surprise that sex stopped being enjoyable. It had been good at first, but her interest quickly faded as he became incredibly demanding. He wanted to have sex three times a day, and he was completely unsympathetic if she was not in the mood. He would hit her, say cruel things, or throw her out of the house.

But the majority of the time she complied, both to avoid violence or further abuse, and because she believed it was her duty, even though she began to find the idea of sex with him disgusting. Although he sometimes hit her to force her to have sex, he never tried to have sex with her after one of his heavy beatings.

Four times he forced her to have sex in front of their child. One day, for example, when they were sitting on the couch while the child was in the room, he kept pushing her head down into his lap and telling her to fellate him. Even under regular circumstances, fellatio turned her off, but with her son there it seemed even more revolting. When she resisted, however, he got mad and smacked her. "It ain't gonna hurt him if he sees it," he said. "Just do it." She did, to keep him calm.

He also compelled her to have anal sex on one occasion. This time she says she went along with it because he made her feel that she was his wife and she was supposed to do what he wanted. "He had me brainwashed," she said.

After he had forced her, she would feel depressed and less like having sex with him. He would become distant and tell her, "Don't come near me. I don't want to see your face." Sometimes after beatings he would apologize, but never after the forced sex.

Although things were getting progressively worse between them and she did leave a few times, she kept coming back. "I had a child and wanted to have a happy family." He made resolutions to change and one time actually got a job; but he didn't change.

During one of their separations, she had an affair with another man, and this drove him to new heights of violence after she returned to him. One night he took a pair of pliers out of the drawer and told her, "I'm gonna rip out your vagina." He made her get on her hands and knees and beg him not to, but then he put the baby on the kitchen counter and said he was going to kill them both.

He was on a rampage. That night he woke her up several times and beat her, and also beat their child. She finally got away and had her mother take her to a shelter her father had told her about. But this did not end her husband's spree: he went to the place where she worked and pulled a knife on the people who worked there, then went to her mother's house and vilified her to her mother. The mother called the police.

At the time we interviewed her, Katherine had filed for a divorce and had made plans to find an apartment. Meanwhile, her husband had told her he had "found the Lord" and was going to church. Thinking he was just playing a game, she would not be fooled into going back. But she was frightened sometimes, worried that he might come and harass her or kill her when she left the shelter. "He's real crazy. You can see the craziness in his eyes. They're red and they're big. It's the weirdest sight to see."

But for the moment she felt great: free and happy. "I'll never go back again. No woman needs to be treated like that."

We asked her if she had ever been raped. "No," she said simply.

Katherine lived in a reign of terror. She learned to swallow her disgust about sex with her husband and comply because it was the way to avoid injury. Her husband was not punishing her through sex so much as asserting his authority and dominance. If she was reluctant to comply, he was not beyond giving her a taste of his violence to bring her around. He was absolutely insensitive to her needs, or even those of their child.

His threat to rip out her vagina was one of the most terrifying incidents recounted in all the histories we took. Consistent with the incredible mania for violence this man displayed, his threat was an attempt to assert his ultimate ownership over her body. Her vagina was his and he would do what he wanted with it. If he could not have it, he was going to ensure that nobody else would, either.

The brutality that is displayed by the husband-rapists we have described in this section is not coincidental. Evidence from other researchers also suggests that among batterers, those who rape are among the most brutal and violent.[5] It appears that there is a continuum of battering, that each batterer has his own limits. Whereas one man will only slap his wife around, another has no compunction about knocking her unconscious, or threatening her with a knife or gun; marital rape is apparently on the more violent end of this continuum.

The conventional stereotype of marital rape disregards the fact that a great many wives are forcibly subjected to a variety of sexual abuses in addition to, or sometimes in lieu of, forced vaginal intercourse. Wives are raped with objects. For instance, one woman's husband tried to rape her with a broomstick and several husbands had their wives insert things in their vaginas and then took pictures of them. Wives are raped anally and their genitals are mutilated. One woman said that her husband would bite her genitals until they bled, and another said she was burned with cigarettes. Wives are forced to have intercourse with their husbands' friends. Two of the women we interviewed said that their assaults had occurred when their husbands ganged up on them with some of their friends. One was able to escape, but the other was not so lucky.

One-third of the women we interviewed mentioned an episode of forced anal intercourse. A fifth told of forced oral sex. Nearly a quarter said they had been subjected to sex in the presence of others—usually their children. These incidents are not disagreements over sexual positions; they are sexual humiliations inflicted on women.

Gretchen was a thirty-nine-year-old woman at the time of our interview; she was born and raised in Germany. She is currently in her third marriage. It was during her first, which lasted only a year and a half, that she was physically brutalized and sexually abused in a way that has left permanent psychological scars.

She was born into a lower-class, rather troubled family. Her father was a factory worker who had lost his leg in the war. She had a brother who was retarded and had to be institutionalized.

Her parents were disciplinarians. Her mother kept a piece of wood to spank the children, and on one occasion had also used a chair for that purpose. Nor were the parents averse to physical altercations between themselves: Gretchen reported that on occasion she "saw some saucers fly" between them.

When she was seventeen, she married a man whom she didn't

really love and who mistreated her badly, and she blames the marriage largely on her war with her mother. Although the neighbor boy she chose seemed to be well mannered, quiet, and good at school, he came from a poor family, and her mother did not like him. In fact, she had forbidden Gretchen to see the boy. "So I just got stubborn," Gretchen told us, and decided to marry him no matter what. She proceeded to get pregnant by him to force the issue.

It was a mistake from the beginning. "A woman with any sense wouldn't marry a guy who had already slapped her around." But she was young and he had apologized profusely, so she decided to take a chance.

The violence continued. At first it was only once a month or so, but gradually it got more and more common until it was happening every couple of days. He wasn't very tall or big but he was strong and had big hands. He left her bruised many times. He would be violent to other people and in front of other people, and their friends just stayed away. One day he beat her up in the kitchen in the middle of a party while their friends were gathered in the living room.

She tried leaving him several times, but he found her and forced her to come back. At one point she managed to get him to see a psychiatrist at a sanitarium for six weeks. When she went to talk to the psychiatrist, however, he told her that "there was absolutely nothing wrong" with her husband, and he could not explain why the man beat her. The psychiatrist recommended that she send him home and come and stay at the sanitarium herself for a few weeks: "You need it more than he does."

The sex, too, was disastrous. She had never enjoyed sex with him, not from the day they married. He took a long time to come, and hurt her during intercourse. He would often beat her and then would want to take her to bed. "I was too afraid to say no. I was afraid I'd get another beating." Sometimes she tried to push him away, but he just persisted until she relented. It got to the point where she was impossibly tense whenever he came near

31

her. At the beginning of the relationship the violence was the worst part, but as the relationship went on, it was the forced sex and the sexual sadism that became the worst. He liked to "play rape": "He wanted me to act like I didn't want him so he could try to force me. That wasn't really hard to do, since it was how I felt. He must have got some satisfaction from hurting me. There wasn't a time when sex with him wasn't violent or painful."

He beat her up and forced her to have sex with him two days before their son was born, and then again two days after. The doctor and nurse wanted to turn him over to the police, but she talked them out of it. "I had just had a baby and I didn't want to raise him by myself." One time she asked her family doctor what was wrong with her husband. "The only thing wrong with him is that he is a sex maniac," the doctor told her. "He needs to have his sexual satisfaction."

"He was possessed," she said in her interview with us, "really possessed. He had this idea that he wanted to pull the insides out of me." He would put his whole hand inside her vagina and try to pull it inside out. Once when he did this he began to hurt her so badly that she kicked him away with her feet. As he pulled away, his fist ripped her vagina, and she started to bleed "like somebody had turned the water on."

A doctor was called, but when he proved unable to stop the bleeding, she was sent to the hospital. As the doctor prepared to sew up the five-to-six-centimeter wound, the husband hit him for touching her genitals ("Nasty as he was, he was jealous, too"). Four blood transfusions later, she recovered, but the doctor told her she had been very, very lucky. Unfortunately, the doctor neither asked about the cause of the injury nor reported it to the police.

Finally she did leave. After she had returned from the hospital and was recovering from this attack, her husband promised never to hit her again, but four weeks later he did. She realized that she might not live through the next beating.

Because he had said he would kill her if she ever left, she hid at the home of relatives for several days. There was one close call, when he almost found her, so she moved to a distant part of the country and took a job under an alias, leaving her one-year-old child behind.

Although she was rid of him, the pain and suffering of that short marriage have dogged her for years. For a long time, she was afraid to go places alone. Even after she remarried and was living in a foreign country, she had visions of his coming back to get her and kill her. The threats he made kept her always on edge. For almost eighteen years afterward, she had nightmares about him.

Cindy, a twenty-six-year-old woman and the mother of two children, aged six and seven, was in school, training to be a bookkeeper when we interviewed her. The man she had married had a long history of delinquency, even as a teen-ager. Thrown out of eighth grade, he had never gone any further in school. He had spent six months in the reformatory, for contributing to the delinquency of a minor (Cindy). He was a foot taller and ninety pounds heavier than she.

He also did not respond very well to the responsibilities of marriage and family. For one thing, he could not find or hold a job, so they lived on welfare and took money from his relatives. He began to get involved in drugs and drank heavily. He went on violent rampages.

"His mind would just snap," she said. "He wouldn't realize what he was doing." One time, in the presence of his brother, he grabbed her by the throat and started choking her. When he let her go, he smashed the cupboards and the windows of their apartment. Another time he held a knife at her throat, right in the middle of his parents' house. His sister passed out and his father "nearly had a heart attack."

Although sexual abuse was virtually a constant in Cindy's marriage, one particular sexual assault stands out above the rest. It happened during one of their periodic separations, a time she had gone off to live with some girl friends to get away from her husband's violence. He and some friends came into a bar where she and her friends were enjoying themselves. They were quite drunk, and she suspected that they had been taking pills, too. When one of his friends kept ogling her and making provocative comments, it surprised her that this did not seem to bother her husband, who was always so jealous.

She left the bar with her friends and went on to a party; again, she was having a good time when her husband walked in, this time minus his lecherous friend. At some point in the evening he asked Cindy if she would go to a nearby apartment to pick up a record that the people at the party wanted to hear. Cindy agreed.

The apartment was dark, but when she went inside somebody grabbed her. It was the friend. As he held her, in walked Jimmy. They held her arms and legs, dragged her upstairs to a bedroom, and ripped off her clothes. The friend took out a pair of brass knuckles and said that if she screamed or hollered he would use them on her. Then they took turns having intercourse with her. "I just laid there and cried. The friend told me, 'If you don't stop your crying I'm going to use them [the brass knuckles] anyway.' " He sounded serious; in fact, it was only her husband's intercession that kept him from doing so. When they were done, her husband said to her, "How'd you like that, you whore? You got two. You just got what you deserved." Then the two of them left, laughing.

After the rape, Cindy felt angry, scared, and confused. She could not understand how her own husband could do something like that to her, and she felt she would like to kill him for it. When she confronted him the next day, he insisted that he thought she had always wanted to have more than one man at a time. "He said he'd always thought of me as a whore and thought I always wanted someone else."

Cindy's experience had all the hallmarks of a typical gang rape: the trickery, the intimidation, the male bonding, the rapists' conceit that they were doing her a favor. This was clearly not just a marital quarrel. "You got just what you deserved," gloated the husband; clearly his motive was to punish and humiliate her.

The most common kind of sexual abuse inflicted on the women we interviewed, however, besides forced vaginal intercourse, was forced anal intercourse. In one-third of the accounts we heard, husbands had either assaulted or attempted to assault their wives in the anus.

Clare is a twenty-four-year-old woman from an affluent background who is currently three years into a second marriage. Her forced-sex experience had occurred with her first husband, to whom she had been married for three years while they were both in college.

The violent sexual episode took place at the very end of the relationship. Things had been deteriorating between them for a long time, to the point where they had not been talking to each other for two weeks. One afternoon she came home from school, silently changed into a housecoat, and started toward the bathroom. He got up from the couch, grabbed her, pushed her down on the floor with her face in a pillow, and, with his hand clamped over her mouth, proceeded to have anal intercourse with her. "It was very violent," she said. Despite the pillow, she screamed so loud that the neighbors heard. But he was very strong and had her pinned down with his full weight on top of her back; and nobody came to help.

When it was over, she found herself distraught, hateful, furious. "If I had had a gun there, I would have killed him," she said.

The victims of anal rape that we interviewed reported a great deal of pain and in some cases long-term damage as a result of these assaults. Clare said that for weeks afterward she had to defecate standing up, and that the injury took five years to heal fully. Another woman said that repeated anal rapes left her rectum torn and bleeding.

At first we were surprised by the number of anal rapes we heard about. But as we understood better the motives of the men who committed these assaults, the frequency of anal rape made more sense.

Raping a woman anally was an act by which the men expressed their anger, their control, and their desire to punish. Most of the women found it deviant and detestable, something they would not have consented to ordinarily.

The act in itself, when imposed by force, emphasizes the passivity, subservience, and impersonality of the victim. The woman takes no active part, as she would in fellatio. The man himself is not vulnerable, as he would be in either cunnilingus or fellatio. Because the man is facing the woman's back, he can avoid confronting her feelings and reactions in a way that would be difficult in ordinary vaginal intercourse. He can treat her as an impersonal object. In many ways, anal rape appears to be the quintessential way for a man to humiliate his wife.[6] This may help account for its frequent occurrence in forced-sex situations.

The image of marital rape as an unfortunate bedroom quarrel needs to be recast to encompass the full spectrum of the reality. Some rapes, of course, *are* little more than bedroom quarrels. But to think of marital rape solely in that way is to misunderstand the horrible reality of many women's experience.

The myths of marital rape obscure both the grisly acts of violence and torture that it can entail and the degree of injury. They do not convey the terror in which many of the victims live. Nor do they adequately convey the motives of marital rape. Marital rape, as we will see in the next chapter, is much more varied than any of the myths would have it.

3

Three Types of Marital Rape

As the previous chapter illustrates, battered women are at high risk for marital rape. The kind of man who beats his wife is also more likely to rape her. If he is not deterred by the social conventions against punching and hitting, he will probably not be inhibited by social conventions against forcing sex, either. We identify this type of forced sex combined with beatings as *battering rape*.

However, even though violent relationships are high-risk relationships, we must guard against replacing the old sanitary stereotype—that marital rape is little more than a marital tiff—with a new stereotype—that marital-rape victims are all battered wives.

In *Rape in Marriage*, Diana Russell warns, "Wife rape cannot and must not be subsumed under the battered women rubric."[1] Indeed, in our study we found that marital rape was not by any means limited to women who were battered.[2] It occurred in relationships in which there was little or no other violence; in relationships of relative sexual equality; and even in relationships where there was little verbal or psychological abuse. We call this second type *force-only rape* because husbands use only as much force as necessary to coerce their wives into sex.

Jessica's marriage was devoid of violence until the night she was raped by her husband. A thirty-six-year-old woman with a master's degree, Jessica had worked for many years as an educational administrator when we talked with her. She had been married and divorced twice. She grew up in a lower-middle-class family, the only child of a Protestant mother and an Irish-Catholic father who was excommunicated as a result of his marriage. She remembers being a happy child, a "goody two-shoes" who, she boasted, had only been spanked once.

She met her first husband when he was in the navy. After a few months of dating, he asked her to marry him. Jessica was "tired of the hassle of dating, tired of the emotional upheaval, and he seemed to love me. So, sure," she said.

Their unconventional, independent marriage lasted five years. He worked on a fishing boat, while she was a teacher. He would be gone for four weeks, then home for four weeks. "I could have lived with Genghis Khan under that arrangement," she said.

Money was the source of some friction: though they both worked hard, they never seemed to get ahead of the game. She became involved with the women's movement and persuaded him to take on more responsibility for housework. Although there were a few heated arguments, these never spilled into any physical violence. (She had told him that she would not stay if he hit her.) When they did disagree, she would retreat to her books and he to his shop.

There was also tension about sex. They had had a fine sexual relationship prior to their marriage, but the instant they got married—the very night, in fact—she decided she did not want to have sex any more: the excitement was gone. Part of the problem was that "I have a stubborn streak eight miles wide. When I feel

I have to do something, I'm much less likely to do it, sex or anything else."

So they fell into a pattern of having sex rarely more than once a month. "I don't think I have a very high sex drive. I want to be hugged and held." She has experienced the same sequence in all the sexual relationships she has had: excitement at the beginning, then a slowing down to about once a month.

When she had been married about a year, she also began an affair that was to last for the rest of her marriage. "It was like being married to two people. I saw him [her lover] every couple of weeks. Strangely, I don't think my marriage would have lasted as long as it did if I hadn't had this other relationship. It provided pieces I wasn't getting from my husband. He understood me better, he was more nurturing, and we had more in common." She never told her husband about it and he never guessed.

The tempo of their sex life did not suit her husband. He was into the service mentality—"get drunk, get laid"—and he thought he was a wonderful lover. She mostly wanted to get it over with. So he had affairs, too.

It was an episode of forced sex that brought the marriage to its close. He had been gone for several days and came home drunk. As they were going to bed, he told her he wanted to have sex with her. She particularly did not like having sex with him when he was drunk, and so she told him she didn't want to. He insisted, pinning her down on the bed and holding her arms. "I was crying and saying, 'No, I don't want to do this.' I was not totally hysterical, but I was real clear. After he forcibly entered me, I just gave up and cried. It was not really possible to resist more. With my arms pinned down and him on top of me, there was just nothing I could do except hurt myself. If he was not going to stop because I did not want to do it, then there was no way I could have stopped it physically. So I just gritted my teeth and said to myself, 'It'll soon be over.' When he was done, he rolled over and went right to sleep."

Afterward she felt violated, enraged. "How dare he do this to me? Although this man had been sexual with me for years, this was different. It really hurt my dignity." She decided that moment to get a divorce, then cried herself to sleep. She remembers it as the most traumatic incident of the marriage.

Why did he do it? She connects it only indirectly to their disagreement over sexual frequency. The more immediate cause, she thinks, is that he had been having an affair with someone for a few days before coming home. "It was his way of erasing what he had been doing. He had a high need to reassert that this was really his primary emotional relationship, and he did that through sex."

They never talked about the incident, either then or later, although they are still friends. "I'm not sure he even remembers it. I'm sure, if he does, he has a different view of it than I do. He'd probably say that he wanted to have sex, that I didn't feel like it, but that I did it anyway. It was not a trauma for him." She thinks he basically believed he had a right to sex, although she is not sure he would say that when sober: "He thought of himself as something of a feminist."

She has told only a couple of other people about it: her second husband and a current lover. Though she would like to be more public about it, especially if there were ever a campaign to change the marital-rape laws in her state, she does not want to humiliate her husband, who still lives in her community.

She saw the incident as a kind of rape from the moment it happened, yet she never considered pressing charges. She would have if it were a beating. But with a rape, "You'd have to tell it all again in front of a bunch of strangers, and sex is not supposed to be something you talk about."

Jessica knew she wanted a divorce, but she did not want a confrontation. So before she asked for a divorce, she made sure he had found another woman to fall in love with; in essence, she says, she manipulated him out of the marriage.

Jessica's story stands in sharp contrast to many of the accounts

40

we have previously cited. Besides being far from a battered wife, she was a professional, an independent woman, and a feminist, and from her description, her relationship with her husband was one of relative equality.

Consider another marriage, quite different.

Harriet is a very well dressed and attractive forty-five-year-old woman who has been living by herself since she divorced her husband four years ago. She had been married for twenty-one years at the time of the divorce and has a grown daughter. Though she was currently looking for work when we interviewed her, in the past she had worked as a lab technician.

Harriet grew up in a small town in a family with six brothers and two sisters. When we asked about her parents, the first thing she said was "My father was a very mean man." He had a good job as a health officer for a large chemical plant, but he drank a lot and frequently abused his wife and children. They all feared him: "When he said 'jump,' you jumped." She remembered being slapped around by him when she was as old as seventeen: she had refused to quit a well-paying job, which he demanded because he claimed it deprived him of a tax exemption.

Her mother was a gentle lady, but she suffered mercilessly from her husband, who at one point knocked her teeth out. As the kids got older, they used to protect her from him, but she never made a move to leave. "My mother was the very old-fashioned type. In her book, a woman doesn't leave her husband."

Harriet met her future husband, Carl, while she was a senior in high school and he was in the military. After two years of dating, they married and settled down in their home town. He went to work in the plant, and she took a job as a lab assistant.

Their early years together were satisfactory, though not all that Harriet had hoped for. She missed the togetherness that she thought a husband and wife should have, and felt she was never able to communicate with her husband. If she tried to talk with him about something serious, he would go to the bedroom, close the door, and go to bed. "It was exasperating. He would never open up."

Harriet's major grievance in the marriage, however, was that Carl never helped her out. "I had too much responsibility. Carl felt all he needed to contribute was his paycheck. Everything else was mine to do." Eventually she became resentful about it. "I never argued or fought with him, because that's the way I am," but as time went on she became increasingly rebellious in her actions. She would refuse to do this or that or say, "It's your turn." "It never got me anywhere, but I just began to rebel."

In the later years of their marriage, this rebellion became more overt. It led, on one occasion, to Carl's becoming quite violent, the only such incident in the marriage. Carl had an annoying habit of lecturing her from time to time, wagging his finger in her face to emphasize his points, and she had told him many times that she did not like it. One evening, as they sat down to dinner, he started his finger-wagging routine. This time she jumped up and started wagging her finger in his face, just to show him how it felt. Furious, he swept the freshly made dinner off the table, overturned the table, then started to throw chairs and dishes around the room, and finally at her. She got hit by some of the flying objects and sustained some cuts and bruises, but she was more emotionally than physically hurt. "He did it because I was defying him," she said.

Their sex life had its ups and downs, but eventually it succumbed to the general deterioration of the relationship. When they were first married, sex was something Harriet did because it was her duty. Carl had been her first sex partner. Since she did not know how to relax or respond, she enjoyed it very little. Carl wanted sex "every time I turned around," sometimes as often as three times a day, and that was much too much for Harriet. She never refused him, though. After the birth of their daughter, which left Harriet very sick for several months, their sexual frequency slowed down a little, but not without a lot of complaining from Carl. He resented the baby, she thinks, because it cut into his sexual "rights."

By the fifth year of marriage, however, Harriet's feelings about sex went through a transformation. She developed the ability to relax and respond, and suddenly she found herself enjoying sex very much. Their sexual frequency increased at that time to about once a day, and it continued that way to their mutual satisfaction for many years.

But it all fell apart in the last two or three years of the marriage. Harriet's resentment had built up by then to such a high level that sex hardly interested her at all. Besides working eight hours a day, she was carrying all the responsibility for the care and maintenance of their home, a burden Carl would not share. "Because of these unfair responsibilities, I lost respect for him. I felt less and less loving toward him, and I can't have sex with somebody I don't feel respect and attraction for."

It was during this period that the first forced-sex episode occurred. "We were in bed, on our opposite sides, and he decided that he wanted to have sex. I said, 'Leave me alone.' But he forced himself on me." Carl didn't hit her; he simply rolled her over on her back, pinned her arms behind her, forced her legs apart, and had intercourse with her. "I was trying to push him away and trying to kick at him. But he is a big man—225 pounds, six feet tall—and I'm five feet two, 110 pounds, soaking wet. So I had to give up. He had full advantage of me within ten minutes."

Though he did not abuse her physically or verbally, he told her not to struggle, for it would not do any good. He did not tear off her nightgown, just hoisted it up to her waist. Intercourse lasted about five minutes.

"It wasn't physically painful and I didn't cry. But I was disgusted, angry, and I hated him."

He told her afterward, "You realize that I raped you. You forced me to do it. You didn't want to have sex with me, so I had to force you." Realizing that he was blaming it all on her, as he did so many things, Harriet stayed very angry at him and started to remove herself more and more from his presence. Shortly thereafter they separated.

One night after moving out, Carl showed up at the house around ten o'clock, on a pretext of needing to get something. Harriet was in her bathrobe and when she came out of the bathroom to go back to bed, he was in the living room taking off his clothes. He had obviously been drinking, and she told him to get out right away. But he said he had decided that she was still his wife and if he wanted her he could have her. "So practically before I knew what was happening, he had grabbed me and dragged me into the bedroom. I was fighting like hell this time, but it got me nowhere." He had sex with her almost exactly the way he had the time before. After he was done, he said nothing. He put his clothes on and left. She glared at him and hated him, but didn't say anything.

She feels she resisted him as best she could on that occasion. She knew he would not hurt her badly, but he had taken her so unexpectedly that she was pinned down and unable either to run or to defend herself before she knew what was happening. There was no one else within earshot, so she didn't bother screaming.

After that incident, he never came back. For her it meant the ultimate loss of any respect or consideration she had ever felt for him. She filed for divorce soon thereafter, though she had hesitated to get a divorce before this, fearing the prospect of having to survive on her own. This incident had convinced her.

Why did he do it? "He was always used to domineering me, having the upper hand in absolutely everything. I had reached the point of rebellion, and he was fighting my rebellion. He was always very possessive of me, jealous, and frequently made wild accusations. I think he regarded me as his possession. It was his privilege to do with a possession whatever he pleased."

Harriet was not an independent, middle-class feminist like Jessica. She was a small-town, working-class homemaker. And while she had a job, she also worked hard to care for her home and daughter. Moreover, Harriet believed she should defer to a domineering husband who insisted on his male prerogatives, whether that meant sex or exemption from household chores.

Harriet was hardly a chronically battered wife: there had been only one violent episode in seventeen years of marriage. Nor was she the victim of continual verbal or psychological abuse. There was no terror, no unpredictable outbursts, little drinking. Yet Harriet, too, was the victim of marital rape.

Jessica and Harriet are not isolated cases. Among the women we interviewed, there were many—about 40 percent—who were victims of force-only rapes. Some had been struck; some remembered nasty, violent episodes; but the violence was unusual, and in some of these relationships it had been on both sides. In any case, these women had not been subjected to the frequent and frightening outbursts that the victims of battering had.

There were other factors besides violence that differentiated the experiences of the victims of force-only rapes and battering rapes. (Statistics about the differences between the victims of these two kinds of rape are in Appendix A, Table 13.) For one thing, the victims of force-only rapes were a much more educated, middle-class group. More of them had been to college, and almost half of them held business or professional-level jobs, whereas very few (only 5 percent) of the battered women had. And many fewer of the victims of force-only rapes (6 percent) came from homes where they had been victims of child abuse.

Type of marital relationships also differentiated the two groups. The victims of force-only rapes were less likely to have been in relationships based on the traditional roles of husband as decision-maker and wife as caretaker. Although both groups were likely to be separated (all but two of our interviewees were separated), the relationships of the victims of force-only rapes had had more durability and had gone on longer before dissolving.

The kinds of sexual assault of the victims of force-only rapes were different, too. For the battered women, rape was a chronic problem that, in some cases, had to be faced every time their husbands wanted sex. Some of them said they were raped twice a week for a period as long as two years. The victims of force-only rapes, on the other hand, faced such long-lasting and continual abuse much less often. In addition, their husbands did not use more force than was necessary to achieve sexual access; the goal was to accomplish the sex act rather than hurt the woman.

The force-only rapes were more often prompted by a sexual conflict, whereas the battering rapes were not usually preceded by any actual conflict over sex. For example, because she had dared slap him, Shirley's husband punched her in the belly and then raped her. As Clare walked toward the bathroom, her husband tackled her and forced himself into her rectum. These rapes appeared to be angry outbursts intended to punish and humiliate, not specifically sexual conflicts.

In the force-only rapes, by contrast, sex was more often at issue. Jessica's husband wanted her to have sex, and when she refused, he forced her. Harriet's husband told her he had to force her because she was unwilling to have sex with him. The men in these relationships more often appeared to be acting on some specifically sexual complaint. In some cases the complaint was a long-standing disagreement over a sexual issue, such as how often to have sex or what were acceptable sexual activities. For example, Mary's husband wanted to have sex every day. Because she wasn't interested that often, he used force. At some point the long-standing disagreement spilled over into coercion. The force-only rapes were not necessarily less humiliating and upsetting, but they less often involved extra violence, and more often involved a specifically sexual grievance.

Nicholas Groth is a prison psychologist who has worked extensively with rapists and other sexual offenders at the Connecticut Correctional Institute. Based on the rapists he has interviewed, Groth distinguishes among the motives that impel men to rape.

46

One important distinction he discusses in his book, *Men Who Rape*,[3] is between anger rapes and power rapes. Although all rapes have elements of both anger and power, anger rapes are committed primarily to express hostility toward women, to retaliate against them, and to humiliate and hurt them. Power rapes, in contrast, are rapes committed primarily to assert dominance and control over women.

Groth's two types of rapes help to distinguish between the types of marital rapes we have described—battering rapes and force-only rapes. The battered women appear to be victims primarily of anger rapes, the nonbattered women of power rapes.

Here is how Groth describes the anger rape:

The assault is characterized by physical brutality. Far more actual force is used in the commission of the offense than would be necessary if the intent were simply to overpower the victim and achieve sexual penetration. Instead, this type of offender attacks his victim, grabbing her, striking her, knocking her to the ground, beating her, tearing her clothes and raping her. His aim is to hurt and debase his victim, and he expresses contempt for her through abusive and profane language. . . . Often this type of offender forces the victim to submit to or to perform additional sexual acts that he may regard as particularly degrading, such as sodomy or fellatio.[4]

This sounds like the kind of assault many of the battered women recount. It is a good description of Grace's husband, who would suddenly hit her in the face in the middle of intercourse. It is also a fitting description of Darlene's husband, who would heap verbal abuse on her while they had sex, calling her an imbecile, a moron, an idiot, "every name in the book." It also describes the spirit with which several of the batterers forced their wives to have anal sex with them, despite the wives' pleas. These men were attempting to hurt, debase, punish, and retaliate against their wives, and they were using sex as another vehicle, along with the physical abuse, to express their anger.

Here is how Groth describes the power rape:

In another pattern of rape, power appears to be the dominant factor motivating the offender. In these assaults, it is not the offender's desire to harm his victim but to possess her sexually. Sexuality becomes a means of compensating for underlying feelings of inadequacy and serves to express issues of mastery, strength, control, authority, identity, and capability. His goal is sexual conquest, and he uses only the amount of force necessary to accomplish this objective.[5]

The assault may be triggered by what the offender experiences to be a challenge by a female or a threat from a male, something which undermines his sense of competency and self-esteem and activates unresolved feelings of inadequacy, insecurity, and vulnerability. He attempts to restore his sense of power, control, identity, and worth through his sexual offense. When one feels there are no other avenues of expression left, there are always the physical resources: strength and sexuality.[6]

Harriet's situation was a perfect example of a power-motivated rape. For months, she had been challenging her husband's control over her, rebelling against his refusal to communicate and his refusal to do his share of the work. Because of the unfair division of labor, she says she lost her respect for him and no longer wished to have sex with him. He must have felt her challenge and decided that he would reassert his control, so he forced her to have sex with him and blamed her for the rape. To maintain his "ownership" of his wife and his power over her, he raped her.

Another story from a victim of force-only rape that fits this pattern of dominance and power was related to us by Sybil.

Sybil was a thirty-three-year-old woman with a four-and-a-half-year-old son. Both she and her husband of ten years, also thirty-three years old, were college graduates and professionals. She taught in a public school and he was a guidance counselor. Their marriage, from her report, seemed to be modern in most respects. They met while in the Peace Corps, and both had fairly profeminist values in political and social matters; family decisionmaking was shared equally. There had been one or two violent episodes in the relationship, but in them there appeared to have been violence on both sides.

There was some long-standing tension in the relationship about sex. He liked to have sex every night, whereas she preferred sex about three nights a week but felt quite a bit of pressure to have more. She said she was afraid that if she refused him he would leave or would force her. Nevertheless, she estimated that their actual sexual frequency was three times a week.

He had forced her to have sex once, about two years before we interviewed her. Their lovemaking on this occasion had started out pleasantly enough, but he tried to get her to have anal intercourse with him. She refused. He persisted. She kicked and pushed him away. Still he persisted. They ended up having vaginal intercourse, but he used his weight, lying on top of her, to force her (he weighed about twice as much as she).

"It was horrible," she said. Sick to her stomach afterward, she cried and felt angry and disgusted. Meanwhile, he showed little guilt; in fact, "He felt like he'd won something."

Why did she think he did it? "He feels like I control when we have sex, and this was showing me that even if I didn't want to, it could happen anyway. . . . I am more afraid of him now." They were still living together at the time of the interview.

When the interviewer asked her, "Have you ever been raped?," she replied quickly, "No," but then she thought for a minute. "I guess, yeah. I guess that incident would be."

In addition to the cases we classified as battering and force-only rapes, we encountered a half dozen that did not fit into either of these categories, that had a bizarre element to them. Sometimes the men in these cases battered their wives, and sometimes they did not. But in all cases, their sexual interests ran toward the strange and the perverse, and they were willing to use force to carry these activities out. We termed this third type *obsessive rape*.

Melanie was thirty-one years old when we talked to her and was employed as a marketing analyst for a large corporation. She described her family background as "very middle-middle class." Her father owned a restaurant and her mother was a teacher while she was growing up. They lived in an ordinary neighborhood and attended the local Protestant church.

Melanie met her husband in high school. He was a bright boy and had skipped a grade, so they were in the same class even though Melanie was a year and a half older than he. His family was much better off socially and economically than hers: his father was the president of a bank, and they enjoyed an affluent life style.

Melanie was attracted to her future husband because he was intelligent, and because he paid attention to her. He was her first boy friend, and she felt flattered by his interest. In the two years that they dated, she thought that he would drop her at some point, though he never did.

While they were dating, he kept pushing for sex until she finally gave in. "I was real passive and easily manipulated at that time. He just wore me down," she said. After they had had intercourse regularly for some time, he began to want to spank her as part of the sex act. This did not appeal to her, but he persisted with his request. Eventually she gave in and let him spank her once; after that he lost interest in doing it again.

In the middle of her senior year, Melanie became pregnant. They decided to get married, but his parents were opposed to the wedding. Since he was under-age, they had to wait until he turned eighteen; Melanie was eight months pregnant when they married.

After the baby was born, he grew more and more demanding sexually. "He was the husband and I was the wife and it was my responsibility to satisfy him. . . . I was really just his masturbating machine," Melanie said. They had intercourse at least twice a day. He seemed to enjoy the sex, but Melanie felt unsatisfied. "He just wasn't warm or sensitive. It was so cold, I can't really call it love-making." She didn't realize how mechanical and unaffectionate he was until years later, after the divorce, when she had a good sexual relationship with another man.

The first incident of physically forced sex occurred one night after he had been out drinking. It was late, and Melanie was doing laundry. He came in and flopped down on the bed—passed out, she thought. She went to the next-door building where the laundry room was to put in another load. As she walked back into the apartment, a man jumped out of the closet, grabbed her from behind, and began to rip off her clothes. At first, she did not even realize that it was her husband. Though she screamed and struggled to get away, he used his superior size and weight to overpower her, tear her clothes off, and rape her anally.

Afterward, he was actually angry with her for being so frightened and for trying to resist. She did not know how to react. "I felt sick and totally disappointed. I had respected him, and had thought we were going to have a good marriage."

After that, he became obsessed with anal sex, demanding it more and more often. He also became more and more forceful during regular intercourse. "He would turn ugly so quickly, especially if I showed any sign of enjoying it. He would put a pillow over my face and I would scream quietly," Melanie remembers. He pressured her into doing bizarre things that made her uncomfortable. He would tie her up, for example, insert objects into her vagina, and then want to take pictures of her. "I was humiliated to find out that he had shown a picture of me with a banana in my vagina to a friend of his."

There were also more brutal attacks. At first these occurred only about once a year, and Melanie made excuses for them and tried to deny them to herself. However, they began to occur more frequently toward the end of their six-year marriage. One incident that stood out in Melanie's mind occurred when they were living in a rural area, in a house quite distant from any neighbors. They were having sex one night when they heard a commotion outside and went in their bathrobes to investigate. Discovering that it was just their cats making noise, Melanie began to head back to the house, but her husband stopped her. "Wait there," he told her, "I'll be right back." She was standing in the darkness wondering what he was up to when suddenly he attacked her from behind. "He grabbed my arms behind me and tied them together. He pushed me over the log pile and raped me," she said. Once again, he penetrated her anally.

After this attack, Melanie was furious. Though he apologized later and expressed remorse, she felt that it was not genuine and that he was not really concerned about her suffering. They argued often about his sexual demands and his brutality. Angry and upset when she resisted, offended when she fought back by scratching or kicking, he complained bitterly and fretted that his injuries (usually scratches) might become infected.

Melanie felt trapped in what she called her husband's "pornographic world." He seemed obsessed with sex. He would talk about it incessantly, evaluating last night's activities at the breakfast table and planning the approaching night at dinner. He was deeply engrossed in all types of pornography: movies, books, magazines. "He read book after book about women being brutalized and victimized." Much of the material was focused on anal sex, she recalls. He was also writing pornographic short stories himself. Melanie once found one in which a woman matching her description was gang-raped. In another story, the same character was murdered by her husband when he came home from work one day.

Finally Melanie confronted her husband directly. Either they would start going to counseling together, she said, or they had to divorce. Within twenty-four hours, he agreed to a divorce, and he moved out of the house shortly thereafter.

A few weeks later, Melanie came across a file card that sickened her. On it her husband had written a list of dates corresponding to the forced-sex episodes of the previous few months. Next to each date was a code. "As close as I could figure it, he had graded each rape on some sort of zero-to-ten ranking, depending, I guess, on how good it was." There were other numbers and letters which she suspects indicated the types of acts he committed. "The card totally stunned me. And it opened my eyes to the fact that he wasn't going to change." She had thought that his attacks had been spontaneous, but it became clear that his behavior was calculated. She was not sure whether he had planned the attacks beforehand or just evaluated them afterward, but she knew that his attitude toward the rapes was much more rational than she ever suspected.

Convinced that the divorce was a necessity, Melanie told her husband that she intended to present the whole story to her lawyer. "He told me that if I *ever* brought up that stuff, he would kill me. I kept thinking about that short story, and I believed him."

Since Melanie's main concern was to get the divorce accomplished, she agreed to let her husband sue her for divorce on the grounds of mental cruelty. In court, she heard him testify that she had not provided him with an adequate sex life. The divorce was uncontested, and he agreed to pay a total of a hundred dollars a month in child support for their three children.

Melanie's husband shared a number of characteristics with other perpetrators of obsessive rapes. His general preoccupation with sex was typical. Another common characteristic among all these husbands was their interest not only in reading pornography but in creating it as well, usually by taking pictures of their wives.

Melanie's husband also had the customary predilection for unusual sexual activities: practicing anal intercourse, inserting objects into his wife's vagina, tying her up. Though none of these activities was rare among the other rapists of women we interviewed, they were particularly common among this group of obsessive rapists. These men may not have "staged" sexual assaults as Melanie's husband did, but all had their own bizarre sexual proclivities.

One thing that stands out strongly in Melanie's story is her husband's apparent relish in activities that caused her torment. The staged rapes aroused him because they frightened her. His taste in pornography ran toward the brutal. This man needed to humiliate his wife in order to enjoy sex. Rape for him was a preferred style of sexual arousal, and he seemed to derive pleasure from inflicting pain. Melanie's husband is a good candidate for the term "sadist." Men like him rape their wives in part because the aggression itself is arousing to them. In fact, in some cases, violence may be essential to their sexual arousal.

Nicholas Groth, who defined a category of sadistic rapists, describes them as follows:

In a third pattern of rape, both sexuality and aggression become fused into a single psychological experience known as sadism. There is a sexual transformation of anger and power so that aggression itself becomes eroticized. This offender finds the intentional maltreatment of his victim intensely gratifying and takes pleasure in her torment, anguish, distress, helplessness and suffering. The assault usually involves bondage and torture and frequently has a bizarre or ritualistic quality to it. Such indignities are accompanied by explicitly abusive acts, such as biting, burning the victim with cigarettes, and flagellation. Sexual areas of the victim's body (her breasts, genitals, and buttocks) become a specific focus of injury and abuse. In some cases, the rape may not involve the offender's sexual organs. Instead, he may use some type of instrument or foreign object, such as a stick or bottle, with which to penetrate his victim sexually.[7]

Indeed, just as Groth describes, several of the men we grouped in this category forced wives to insert objects into their vaginas. Several husbands tried to bite, gouge, or damage their wives' genitals in some way.

In using the Groth categories, it is important to understand the difference between anger rapists and sadistic rapists, both of whom inflict pain in a sexual situation. The anger rapists, who are angry and want to punish their wives, use sex as a way of hurting their victims. The sadistic rapists, by contrast, hurt their victims not to punish them but as a way of arousing themselves. Another distinguishing feature of sadistic rapists is the ritualistic quality they bring to their brutality. The sadistic types act almost as though they are staging a show. Certain acts and gestures are essential to their performance.

Although Groth's analysis of the sadistic rapist is extremely useful, his description did not entirely capture the character of all the marital rapes that we grouped in this last category. Several of the men were very much as he describes—deriving pleasure from actual acts of brutality and torment. Yet several others did not seem to be aroused by the pain or suffering they caused but actually by the perverse acts in which they forced their wives to engage.

Ursula was a fifty-year-old woman with a master's degree in anthropology who worked as a museum curator. She had three grown children and was divorced from her husband after thirty years of marriage. Articulate and introspective, she had spent considerable time (and money) trying to understand her marriage.

She grew up in a middle-class Jewish family. Her father, a realtor, had a salesman's outgoing, friendly, and hard-working personality. She was not so close to him, however, as she was to her mother—an attractive, intelligent woman, but somewhat neurotic. Mother and father fought a lot, and Ursula, who was the youngest of three children, was often left to go her own way.

While in college, she met her future husband through an aunt who fixed them up. He was an attractive, smart man, six years older than she. Knowledgeable about jazz, classical music, and other things she liked, he was also a good dancer, and "he had a style I found very appealing."

But from the beginning the marriage did not give her what she wanted. He was very difficult to live with, very domineering and demanding, and "he was much too tied up with his mother." His mother was a dynamic, shrewd, and clever woman, emotionally powerful and controlling. For a year after he and Ursula got married, they lived with the mother, while he worked in her insurance business. "His mother used him. He is tangled up with her and he did the same to me. That's the origin of our problems . . . and the fact that I married him, of course."

She feels that because he was dominated by his mother, he had a great need to dominate his wife. He made all the decisions. He never told her how much money he made, and he gave her no say in financial matters. "As long as I was around him, I couldn't run my own life. He always put me down. I never heard him say something nice about me."

And he had a violent temper. When he got angry, which was frequently, he would "say anything." He would also throw things through the window. "We should have had the glass repairman on a retainer. I think it was a substitute for me." He did knock her around a couple of times (for reasons she cannot remember), and he was extremely domineering and unkind toward their children, acting like a "top sergeant" with them. She has a hard time forgiving him for that.

There were elements of his sexual behavior that she describes as "bizarre." One of the reasons she wanted to be married was to have sex in a socially sanctioned situation: "Here I was jumping into marriage to escape a bad name" and he surprised her by having little sexual drive. They slept in separate beds, and he was not particularly affectionate. She felt lucky if they had sex once every other week. During a month-long vacation, they had sex only two times. Nor did he like her to initiate sex; he said he hated aggressive women.

He also had chronic problems with impotence, virtually from the beginning, needing her to perform oral sex on him in order to arouse himself; many times he could not perform at all. All this was making her very frustrated.

Then he began to get into pornography. Once he found that he could use it to get himself aroused so that he could have sex with her, he began to collect quite a bit of it, including some homosexual pornography. "It got to the point where that was all he read."

Next he wanted to get into swinging, to use her as bait so that he could have relationships with other men and women. Though she did not cooperate with this, he eventually developed a sexual relationship with another couple, having sex with the two of them.

He began to want to use Ursula to make his own pornography, taking pictures of her in "every possible manner." Usually he would get her drunk to encourage her to participate. Once he made a moving picture of her masturbating with a bottle in her vagina. "I had an initial reluctance, but somehow I went along. There was some sexual excitation I got out of this stuff, but I also went along because I didn't know what it was like to have a nor-

57

mal relationship. I used to say to him, 'I don't know how you can love me and have me do these things,' and he would reply, 'Oh, you're so square. . . . You and your morals and ethics, I'm sick of it.' He didn't love me, really, he possessed me, and I didn't know I had any other option."

One thing that particularly disturbed Ursula was that he would enjoy parading around exhibitionistically in front of their daughter, who was approaching puberty. The daughter did not like it, and "it was making me crazy." But he kept it up in spite of her complaints. Only after she complained to his psychiatrist did it stop.

"Every step of the way I had to get pushed. I would think, 'That's crazy and unnatural,' but eventually he'd break me down and I'd go on to the next step. I was starved for love and sex, so I got into it. But it was the downfall of the marriage. That stuff ultimately finished off my feelings for him. It was so bizarre and unnatural."

Although he dominated her and pressured her into sexual activities she found uncomfortable, only on one occasion did he actually use brute physical intimidation. This occurred one night after they had been out to a party at which she had been enjoying dancing and being close with another man. When they got home he was extremely angry, and extremely excited sexually. He stormed into her bedroom and told her, "If you're going to act like a whore, you're going to be a whore to me." She saw that he was stimulated by treating her angrily, which terrified her. "I didn't want to have sex, but I knew that there was no way I was going to stop him."

She did not resist, believing that he would have forced her in any event. "He came on in a way that made me feel that he would use force. I didn't say, No, get the hell out of here, like I should have. I just let him do what he wanted. It was connected in part to a lack of self-esteem."

Afterward, she felt defeated and degraded, too ashamed to tell anyone about that incident or any of their other sexual activities until many years later. Eventually, after the kids had grown up and left home, she did leave the marriage. He had come into the kitchen one morning "stark naked" and demanded to know what she had been up to the previous day. "You're going to tell me who you were with and then I'm going to fuck you," he shouted. He pushed her up against the sink and threatened that when he got back from the office, she was going to get it. Seriously frightened, Ursula left home, took shelter at a friend's house, and made the decision not to go back.

"Basically he is a man who doesn't like women. He doesn't respond to normal things. Only artificial stuff. He has to be in control. He can't function if he's not in control. I don't understand men who need to do that."

Ursula's husband might be classified as a sadist, like Melanie's husband. In using physical force, he was working up a rage in order to enhance his sexual arousal. For the most part, however, he used less physical coercion, instead pressuring Ursula with challenges and insults. Furthermore, the sexual activities he preferred, though pornographic and unusual, were not necessarily aggressive and tormenting. And, unlike the situation with Melanie's husband, his abuse of his wife was characterized not by enjoyment of inflicting pain but by a preoccupation with perverse sexuality.

In characterizing this third category of marital rapes we decided to emphasize the element of obsession rather than the element of sadism. The element of sadism is certainly there in many of the cases, and we think Groth's characterization applies to most of these men. But it is the element of obsession, not sadism, that stood out as the most common feature of this final category of marital rape. We expect that other types of marital rape may be revealed after further studies of the victims and perpetrators of marital rape. However, the major point of this chapter will remain: that marital rape occurs in different kinds of relationships and takes different forms. To characterize marital rape as the province of battered women alone is not to see its full scope. Unfortunately, as we have shown, marital rape occurs in relationships that give fewer signs of "violence" than most of us would surmise.

4

Men Who Rape Their Wives

What kind of man would rape his wife? We were fortunate enough to obtain the testimony of three men who all admitted they had used force at some time to have sex with their wives. All three volunteered to be interviewed after one of us spoke before their community service group. There was quite a variety of reasons for their participation—guilt about what they had done, a desire to unburden themselves to someone, the wish to help out in a study whose intent was to understand and combat family violence. One man volunteered in order to challenge what he saw as some of the study's assumptions.

Although they committed marital rapes, these men were not typical of the husbands we heard about from the women we interviewed. First of all, none of them was a chronic batterer, subjecting his wife to frequent, bullying physical punishment. Second, all three felt some degree of remorse for what they had done. Finally, all of them were middle-class: rather ordinary men, in fact, the kind of people we might expect to meet in everyday life—like our corner druggist, our insurance agent, our lawyer, or our teacher. The relationships they talked about were the kind of relationships we see going on all around us. They were disappointed and unhappy over ordinary things. Their fights and conflicts were ordinary fights. In this respect they resembled only a small number of the men whom our women interviewees described to us.

They were surprisingly forthcoming in describing their behavior, and also willing to be introspective about why they had done what they did. Of course, they were defensive about some matters, and at times they offered what seemed to us flimsy rationales for cruel behavior. But, considering that they were talking to an interviewer who did not approve of their behavior, they were all astonishingly frank. In fact, these three men talked less self-consciously about the rapes they had committed than did many of the victims of rape to whom we talked.

Because they were so frank, and because accounts of marital rape from the perpetrator's point of view are so unusual, we have decided to present their accounts in detail. They help show how marital rape can be an outgrowth of seemingly ordinary marriages, and they lend credence to many of the observations made by the women we talked to.

Ross, a thirty-eight-year-old man, had been divorced for a year and a half when we spoke to him, after a marriage that lasted through thirteen years and two children. He still talked about the divorce in very bitter terms.

A big man with an oddly deferential manner, he was college-educated, a former insurance agent, and, at the time of our interview, trying to get his own business off the ground. He was articulate and showed a fair amount of self-awareness.

Ross grew up in a family that operated under a model of absolute obedience to the father. His father, an engineer from a first-generation Austrian background, was stern and demanding. "There was no such thing as a job well done," Ross remembered.

"My problem growing up was that no matter what I did, it wasn't good enough for my father." His father had a temper and was swift to discipline. Ross remembered one evening at the dinner table when, having been told not to interrupt the adults' conversation, he reached a bit too far to get the salt. His father, who was carving meat, suddenly smacked him hard on the hand with the back of the carving knife. This image of his father hitting him with a knife is imprinted on Ross's memory.

His mother fitted somewhat the same mold. Descended from minor Austrian nobility, she had an "exaggerated notion of aristocracy," with all the prejudice and snobbery that went along with it. She was always urging him to achieve. "More, more, more" was her message. To compound matters, he had an older brother who bested him at everything and, when he couldn't win fairly, would beat Ross up. It was hardly an environment to give one much sense of self-confidence or self-esteem. Nor was it an environment for learning anything about girls. There were only boys in the household and only boys in the neighborhood. "I didn't get to know girls as human beings until high school," Ross said.

He met his future wife, Tania, on a blind date when he was about to finish high school. Instantly head over heels in love, he committed himself to her blindly from then on. He dogged her throughout college, though they were separated by many miles. While he stayed true to her, she dated many other men. "From the very beginning, the whole relationship was always totally on her terms. I had little confidence." But Ross's persistence and forgiveness paid off: shortly after finishing college, she agreed to marry him.

He was not exactly welcomed into her family. Tania's father was rich, a self-made man who had married his much younger secretary. He was quite unstable, drank a lot, and did not try to conceal from his family his affairs with still younger women. He had also, as Ross found out later on, sexually abused Tania when she was ten. The father took no liking to Tania's suitor. On one occasion, the father had tried to physically eject him from the house. What was probably the jealousy of an incestuous father, Ross took to be class snobbery. "I wasn't good enough because I didn't go to Yale or Harvard" was the message he got.

Although he says that knowing about her family background helps him to understand his wife and her relationship to him, he has little compassion for her. From the beginning he felt that their marriage was a struggle for control. "She wanted to control everything. She wanted the last word about all issues. I picture her as having a kind of plastic shell around herself. Her whole character was nothing but taking care of herself regardless of the cost to anyone else." If he wanted to go out, she didn't. If he wanted to paint the porch tomorrow, she wanted it painted today. He describes an endless battle of wills, which he felt she ultimately won.

Not surprisingly, their war spilled over into the bedroom. "She had me completely and totally emasculated. She told me she couldn't be sexually interested in me unless I'd done something to earn it" (in other words, unless he started making more money). "She told me that she realized that there was no one man who could give her enough attention to make her happy. She had this very young girl's Victorian picture of sex, where the man did all of this heavy courting, where the lights were just right and there was music and flowers and the whole nine yards. All she had to do was lie there."

He feels he made an exceptional effort to satisfy her. "I think she was lucky. Ninety-nine percent of the time she climaxed, and I had to work damn hard at it, even to the point where I lost interest," he boasts. But he thinks she was not appreciative of his effort. She had a take-it-or-leave-it attitude toward sex, and never once, in thirteen years of marriage, took the initiative sexually. Sometimes when he was aroused and they were in the middle of foreplay, she would stop and tell him she wasn't interested. "She might just as well have taken a knife and chopped my balls off."

Ross's concern about his sexual adequacy was not entirely new. He remembered that he was late to mature as a boy, and it embarrassed him for many years to be in the locker room with boys his age. Later in life he found a survey in *Forum Magazine* on penis size and he established, much to his relief, that when erect he was a little bit bigger than average. "It did great things for my self-esteem. When I'm flaccid, I all but disappear."

Early in their marriage, Tania caught him masturbating and told him she thought it was awful. But later on, when she wasn't interested, she would tell him to go ahead and do it. As their marriage wore on and sexual frequency declined to once every four or five weeks, he was masturbating more and more. He also had some sporadic affairs, only one of which she ever found out about.

But one of his main ways of expressing his sexual dissatisfaction was through fantasizing, especially about somebody else having sex with Tania while he watched. "I was feeling inadequate," he explains, "and I think I believed that maybe someone else could satisfy her." When he made what he sees as the fatal mistake of sharing this fantasy with her, she was repulsed and didn't want to have anything to do with it, although he thinks that she may have strung him along a little with the vague possibility that she might agree. For the most part, she threw it back in his face as a sickness or kinky tendency.

He held on to the fantasy, however, and it got stronger. "I got to the point where I could only keep a sexual interest in her through this fantasy. Given the Victorian attitude she took about her body, a liberal sexual attitude was the only way I could get the better of her."

Ross began to use the fantasy as a kind of punishment. "If I was really pissed at her, it gave me a certain degree of pleasure to get her into bed and get her going. Then I would start fantasizing." Sometimes he would tell her about the fantasy as he was having it. "It gave me a certain feeling of power over her, because I knew she found it unpleasurable. It was one of the only times I could best her."

Eventually his antagonism broke out in even more coercive

ways. "On one occasion we were having a fight, and for some reason she was standing there in her nightie. The whole thing got me somewhat sexually stimulated, and I guess subconsciously I felt she was getting the better of me. It dawned on me to just throw her down and have at her . . . which I did. I must have reached out and grabbed at her breast. She slapped my hand away. So I said, 'Lay down. You're gonna get it.' She replied, 'Oh, no, you don't,' so I grabbed her by the arms and she put up resistance for literally fifteen seconds and then just resigned herself to it. There were no blows or anything like that. It was weird. I felt very animalistic, and I felt very powerful. I had the best erection I'd had in years. It was very stimulating. She cried and carried on afterward. I guess I felt some shame when I looked down on the floor and saw her sobbing. But I knew she wasn't physically hurt. After that she wouldn't let me into the bedroom, and she called me every name in the book. I'm not proud of it, but, damn it, I walked around with a smile on my face for three days. You could say, I suppose, that I raped her. But I was reduced to a situation in the marriage where it was absolutely the only power I had over her."

Ross said the forced sex recurred twice in the last two or three years of their marriage. On these occasions, she did not resist as much as the first time. "There wasn't all the tears and bullshit. Just anger and loathing." On these occasions, too, he said he felt "great."

"Subconsciously I think she kept egging me on because she wanted to be dominated. You know, when you are accosted by someone in the street who tries to take your wallet and you knock them out, the more power to you. It's a just cause. Well, when you get into a marriage, it can be a just cause, too. Like in my situation, she just completely emasculated me. It was the only thing I had left."

They both knew that their marriage was not in good shape. He went to counseling with her, mostly at her urging ("I wish I had all the money we spent on therapy"), but they made little headway. He thinks she refused to listen to what the therapists were saying. "She took the attitude, 'Don't confuse me with the facts.' "

The episodes of forced sex never came up in the counseling, although he is fairly sure that she told others about them: "She was always on the horn to someone." In fact, she may have even told his parents. She definitely told his parents about his sexual fantasy and about the one time in their marriage when he hit her. "Frankly, she has completely destroyed my relationship with my parents. It will never be the same."

Ross was the one to take the initiative to leave, though he had been afraid to move out because his kids were so important to him. "I knew I would lose them, and I had doubts about just how they would be if I left them with her. But eventually it got to a point where there was so much conflict it was completely tearing me apart inside." He was afraid something dangerous would happen. In fact, "I found myself literally planning ways to kill her, which I would have never done. But when I found it was fun to think about it, I felt really weird about it. I finally came to the conclusion that it would be better for the kids and me if we just split." So he moved into his own cabin, and ended up getting joint custody of the kids.

Still, "I felt very cheated. I didn't get out of a wife and life what I wanted." She suffered, too, he thinks, from a sense of having failed, though she found a new man and got married. Her new husband was thirty-two, but had never before married or had a driver's license and had lived with his mother all his life. "He's the perfect partner for her," said Ross, "somebody she can control."

In forcing his wife to have sex, did Ross think he had committed a crime? "No, I wouldn't have considered it rape at the time. I never thought about it that way until that meeting where I heard you speak."

If he had thought about it as a crime, would it have affected his behavior? "Oh, sure. She would have loved to have run off and have me committed. I wouldn't have wanted to give her that."

Still, Ross is not very enthusiastic about a new marital-rape law. "I can see a lot of women taking advantage of it. My guess is that only 5 to 10 percent of reported incidents would be legitimate. The rest would be a woman taking advantage of a law on the books. Some would just make a story up. Some would vastly blow a situation out of proportion. I think too many women use sex as a weapon already. Why give them another round for their arsenal? It's the ultimate weapon. Since a woman's ultimate weapon is sex, a man's ultimate weapon has to be his strength."

Ross's story is a clear example of what we called earlier a force-only rape. There was little physical abuse, little brutality, and little general intimidation. On the other hand, there were long-standing underlying sexual problems, which culminated in the rapes. The main underlying theme seems to be one of power and control.

Ross was a man who had a history of feeling inadequate in the face of the masculine ideals he held up for himself. Consistent with the dictates of his anxieties, he believed it was particularly important to be in control in his marriage. He saw his wife's refusal to submit to him as a struggle for power that, according to his standards, he invariably lost: "She wanted to control everything. She wanted to have the last word about all issues." He regarded her assertions of power as another attack on his fragile masculine identity, only reinforcing the verdict of his many other defeats.

His sensitivity about sex made that a central battlefield. "She had me completely and totally emasculated," he said. Although it is likely that his wife had plenty of sexual scars herself from her incest victimization by her father, Ross interpreted almost all of her difficulties as intentional slights to his pride. She wanted to deprive him not just of sex, but also of the satisfaction of feeling like a good lover and—by attacking his fantasy of a threesome—

the satisfaction of feeling like a properly liberated twentieth-century sex partner.

When he felt his power and control over her had run out in other spheres, Ross tried doggedly to maintain it through sex. He got a sense of power from having sex with her, from making her reach orgasm—especially in the face of some reluctance—and from using the detested fantasy to his own pleasure in spite of her.

The rape was one more way to win the power struggle, to confirm his masculinity, and to take some revenge, all at the same time. It satisfied many of his needs, and it is not surprising that he walked around with a smile on his face for three days.

In a relationship marked only by a power struggle and not so much by sexual conflict, perhaps the husband would have asserted his dominance in some other way—a slap, a put-down, an arbitrary decision on where to live. But because Ross had a particular sensitivity to sexual rejection and a long-standing preoccupation with sexual adequacy, sex was the arena through which he chose retaliation. He felt wronged, cheated, and deprived in the sexual realm. Rape seemed the appropriate means of revenge.

One can see how much assistance and comfort Ross drew from the male myths about rape. Since rape for Ross was unquestionably a masculine act, it put him in a camp with the kind of masculine man he wished somehow he could be. "I'm not proud of it," he says, "but damn it . . . " But he *was* proud of it, and he almost savored calling it "rape" and taking the credit. He also believed, like many men, that rape really does no great harm. He "knew she wasn't physically hurt," and her crying and anger seemed to him silly and out of proportion to the minor indignity he believed she had suffered. Finally, he appeared to agree with the reigning male stereotype that women really want to be dominated and that violent retaliation is justified by a certain degree of provocation. Though these may have been post-hoc rationalizations, he said she egged him on and got what she deserved.

It is interesting to look at why Ross objected to the idea of criminalizing marital rape. Although he had a particular self-interest in immunity for the husband-rapist, it is likely that his logic would strike a sympathetic chord in the minds of men who don't rape, too. Many men see sex with their wives as a tug of war. Even if they would never use force, the possibility of doing so may be their hidden trump. Don't take that away from me, they protest.

But Ross admitted that, had prosecution been a consequence, he might not have raped—which is honest testimony from a rapist about the potential deterrent value of eliminating the spousal exemption.

Jack, age thirty-three, was a big man, over six feet tall and weighing more than two hundred pounds. Yet, he had a gentle manner: soft-spoken and deferential, he talked very earnestly. One felt that he was struggling hard to be honest and open, and that he very much wanted to be liked. He was, in fact, such a nice, average guy that after meeting him it was much easier to say with conviction that almost any husband can be a rapist.

Jack was recently separated from his wife after twelve years of marriage. College-educated, he was the owner of a small trucking firm. He readily talked about his abusiveness as though the interview were a chance to purge himself and gain absolution. Appearing remorseful about what he had done to his wife, and very ready to admit his errors, he also seemed to be trying very hard to understand how and why it happened.

The eldest in a family of four children, Jack had a father who was also in the trucking business. He regarded a number of his problems as having their source in his family. "My parents do not show their emotions, and they would not let me show my emotions. That's where my problems come from." His parents' marriage was full of conflict. His father, he felt, was always putting his mother down, especially when business was going badly. Still, though they had a couple of hair-raising physical fights, the abuse was for the most part more verbal than physical.

The father took some of his frustrations out on the kids, too, and not just verbally. Jack says he was thrashed many times, at least every other week when he was younger. His father was still doing this when Jack was thirteen: he remembers his father taking a belt to him once when he had hurt his younger brother in a playful game.

Perhaps the major problem with his childhood, however, was that it ended too soon. By age nineteen he was married and the father of a son, and had all the responsibilities of a family to support. His wife, Sylvia, was a year younger than he. Though they had been in high school together and she had admired him from afar as a star on the basketball team, it was not until his freshman year in college that they met, introduced by a mutual friend; they quickly took a liking to each other. He enjoyed her because she was fun and had a great sense of humor. She was also shy and insecure, but Jack was less aware of this in their early days together.

Her mother was a very loving person, but Sylvia's early life was difficult and lonely. Her father had deserted the family when she was eight, and her mother, who had to go to work, had shipped Sylvia off to stay with relatives for a couple of years.

Early in their relationship, Jack and Sylvia started having sex. The first time was great, he said. A week later, however, she didn't want to do it again, so he forced sex on her in the back of a car, in the first of what was to become a long series of rapes. When, soon thereafter, she got pregnant, marriage seemed the only choice.

Jack thought he would have married Sylvia even if she hadn't gotten pregnant, but he was not so sure that she would have done the same. She came from a Catholic family, and "In those days there wasn't any alternative: you got a girl pregnant and you got married. We went right from the nest into marriage."

"It was nice at first, in those early days, being with someone who really cared about me, but there was a lot of resentment on my part for having to get married," Jack remembered. He was trying to finish college—"not so much for me as for her and my family"—and trying to support his young family. "It was tough, and I resented that she could not participate in the financial end. The resentment came out in forced sex."

From the beginning their sexual relationship was not to his liking. "Her attitude toward sex was 'You don't do it.' I had to do a lot of work to talk her into it. She'd say she was in the middle of her cycle, or that she had cramps, or that she was too tired. Or she'd simply stay up until after I went to bed." He also didn't feel she ever told him clearly what she wanted and didn't want. "Sometimes she'd say yes, and sometimes she'd say no. I felt there was no way of knowing what she really wanted because she would not tell me." She didn't have an orgasm for the first eight years of their marriage—something that made him feel very inadequate. Also, he wanted sex at least three nights a week, and that was too often for her.

"When she would not give it freely," Jack admitted, "I would take it. That's as honest as I can get." He guessed that such forced-sex episodes occurred once a month or more throughout virtually the whole of the marriage. Generally, it would start out when they were in bed together. He'd reach out for her, wanting to have sex, and sometimes she'd come willingly. Other times, however, she would tell him she didn't want to or roll farther away. This would make him angry, make him feel, "You can't deny me. I have a right to this. You're not satisfying my needs." He never said this to her, however. Instead he would grab her, roll her onto her back, and hold her down. Though she would struggle sometimes or strike out at him, she was very small and no match for him. A couple of times he slapped her to get her to comply, but usually she would give up before he had to resort to this and let him have his way. He came very quickly. Then she would get up and go into the other room, wash, and perhaps come back to bed. A few times she cried. A few times she called him a bastard. But throughout most of their marriage, he guessed, she felt that she had an obligation to him and just accepted it as her burden.

After a night when he had forced her, she would be cold and distant for a few days, avoiding him around the house, until he reached out to her and apologized. At that point she would forgive him.

Toward the end of their relationship, the sexual conflict grew more bitter. She stopped wanting to have sex at all, and he found he was forcing her, on average, once every other week. Sometimes she would scream out as they struggled, and a couple of times their twelve-year-old son heard her and shouted, "Dad, stop it." Also, as time went on, she was less willing to forgive him, and Jack said there were occasions when he really feared for his life. He had fantasies of her getting a knife and stabbing him while he slept.

Although he realized that he was being brutal to her, he was still certain that sometimes when he forced her to have sex she ended up enjoying it. Even though he had manhandled her at first, she would get aroused as he penetrated her, and end up cuddly and playful afterward instead of angry and resentful. These occasions confused Jack; he couldn't tell when forcing her might be OK. Sometimes "she'd say no and mean yes, and sometimes she'd say no and mean no. It was tough for me to understand what was when. I think that sometimes women want a man to be a brute with them." He said he had recently gotten a confirmation of this idea while reading Nancy Friday's book *Men in Love*. "I am sure that Sylvia wanted me to take responsibility for sex because of her own inhibitions and inability to feel comfortable."

The forced sex resulted in a few pregnancy scares. They had used many different contraceptive techniques after they had two children, but toward the end had settled on condoms. However, he forced her sometimes without wearing one, even when he knew she had a chance of getting pregnant. "I was damn sure I didn't want any more children, but I remember just being angry enough that I decided, 'I'm going to take the risk anyway.' "

Although their sex life together did not improve, they found a way of relieving some of the tension for a while by starting a mate-swapping arrangement with a couple with whom they were very good friends. Although Sylvia had refused to participate at first, once Jack convinced her to try it, they both enjoyed the excitement and the variety for a time. "Looking back on it, it was a lot of fun," Jack remembered. "But after a while I got terribly jealous and wanted to stop it. I thought Sylvia was seeing the other guy outside of the time when the four of us were getting together. I was continually accusing her of stuff during the last months of the marriage. I now realize that nothing was happening between them. But I think my continual accusations were a big factor in the marriage breaking up."

Sylvia began to act more independently and was increasingly rebellious about Jack's behavior. One night he tried to make her have oral sex with him. "I forced her to go down on me, and she retaliated by biting my penis. It hurt a lot. While I was dealing with the pain, she ran off into the bathroom. Then she went to the neighbors' and stayed away."

Her new independence bothered him. He felt she was playing around, having a good time, while he was shouldering all the financial burdens of the family. He asked her many times to get a job, but, lacking self-confidence and job skills, she never did.

It was during an argument over her getting a job that they had their last and most violent fight. Her insolence and defiance had been making him increasingly angry. "I was feeling like I could have killed her. I knocked her down with a slap. She got up and started hitting me. I knocked her down again. Then I felt this urge." It really frightened him, because he had never felt so much anger. "I knew I could really hurt her."

Sensing his potential for violence, she screamed out for help from their son, who was upstairs. The boy didn't come to her rescue, but he did walk tentatively to the top of the stairs, and this, plus his own astonishment at the dangerous feelings he had unleashed in himself, seemed to hold Jack in check. He backed off and stopped hitting her.

Sylvia got up and said she was leaving. After packing her

things, she went to the local women's shelter, where she stayed for three weeks. Before long, she fell into a severe depression, for which she spent ninety days in the hospital. Though they went to counseling together, it did not help. Now they were living apart, and both had sued for divorce.

At the time of our interview, Jack was thinking that he might like to get back together with Sylvia, and that she might like to try a reconciliation, too. But he felt he had changed a lot during their separation, and he was not sure she had. Unless he recognized some kind of change, he was not sure it would work out. "Our marriage had a lot of good in it. I feel strongly about her in a lot of ways. She was a good mother and a good partner; we had a lot of fun together. But she's never really been on her own. That's what kept her with me all that time. I've still got a lot of anger inside me about the marriage. I think my anger comes from having to be perfect. That's what was expected of me all through my child-hood, and that's the way it was in my marriage. I was playing a role, and I don't think I was getting anything back from it. She expected me to work my ass off for her, and I didn't see anything coming from her. She was getting a lot of playtime and I wasn't. I don't think that's selfish on my part."

He thought that the forced sex was his way of expressing his frustration. "It was an excuse to let off steam. I know now I don't need sex three times a week. But it was a way to let out the anger that I'd been holding back from other stuff. I guess I thought then that I had a right to it. I don't feel that any more. Thinking about some of the horrible things I did, I realize they weren't right. Now I'd say it was rape."

But even if Jack had realized that it was rape and illegal back then, he was not sure it would have changed his behavior. More-over, he was confident that Sylvia would never have resorted to the law.

In general, he opposed making marital rape a crime. "I see too much potential for a wife to use it to get even with a guy." He favored alternatives like restraining orders, which his wife had used on him.

When asked what advice he would give to a woman in his wife's situation, he said quickly, "I'd tell her to get out."

In our typology, Jack's rapes would also be considered force-only rapes. His account includes but one incident of serious violence, at the very end. Nonetheless, Sylvia's experience had characteristics in common with those of some of our battered wives—an early marriage, a violent episode (the rape) that occurred prior to the marriage, and a kind of entrapment brought on by her child-care burden combined with her lack of job, schooling, or money.

Like Ross, Jack was suffering from a burdensome conception of the male role. When his girl friend got pregnant, he did the manly thing: he married her, and then he shouldered the responsibilities of breadwinner, achieving student, good father. Unlike Ross, he had confidence that he could do it, but he resented having to. His resentment came to focus on Sylvia, who was, in his mind, at the root of his predicament. Her lightheartedness, which he once liked so much, came to be the symbol of the freedom from care that he no longer had. "I resented that she could not participate in the financial end. The resentment came out in forced sex."

But Jack's story also illustrates the dynamics of another masculine conceit: the belief in *entitlement*. He felt entitled to sex in his marriage when he wanted it. "I have a right to this" was his first reaction when he was rebuffed. It wasn't just that sex was his right by marriage; it was his right as soon as Sylvia became his girl friend.

Early in their marriage, Sylvia would probably have agreed with Jack's view of his sexual rights, at least to some extent. But what made her clearly a rape victim was that sometimes Sylvia put up a fight and Jack used physical force. She would struggle or strike out at him, and once or twice he slapped her to make her comply.

Yet her resistance clearly lacked conviction, and more often than not she would comply without a struggle.

Jack claimed that Sylvia had sexual problems, that she was frigid and inhibited, and his rape was a response to this. It is curious, though, that whatever inhibitions Sylvia had did not prevent her from becoming involved in swinging. Here, too, she may have been the victim of Jack's intimidation. The research on swinging shows that men often use a great deal of pressure to get their wives to go along with them, and then, like Jack, many become disturbed and jealous when their wives seem to derive some pleasure from it.[1] But a more important observation concerning Sylvia's sexual reticence is that perhaps she had reasons to feel cold about his sexual attentions. After all, he had forced her to have intercourse on a date, which resulted in pregnancy and marriage. It is easy to imagine how an early experience of this sort might have made it difficult to feel relaxed, open, and comfortable about sex.

This story is also a poignant illustration of the potential trauma to children that may result from exposure to a sexually assaultive marriage. Jack reported that his son sometimes heard his mother crying out when she was struggling to resist, and the boy would shout to his father to stop. It was not clear whether the boy really knew the details of what was going on, but one can easily imagine how his fears could surpass even the reality of the situation. Though we know very little about what kinds of scars such exposure might cause, it is not hard to believe they could be great and long-lasting.

Paul was a forty-six-year-old chemist who had heard one of us talk about family violence at a social-club meeting and responded to our request for volunteers because he thought he had had "a few experiences that might be of interest." A short, very soft-spoken, and meticulous man, he came to the interview in a three-piece, pin-striped suit. He had been married twice and was in the process of being divorced for the second time. He had three young children who were at the moment the subject of an acrimonious custody dispute with his second wife.

The younger of two children, Paul grew up in a small town. His father, a moody, rugged laborer who worked in the mills and factories of their area and kept a small farm on the side, hadn't gone to grade school and was ill at ease with the complexities of the world. According to Paul, his mother was in charge of the family. She was the one who told Paul's father "where to turn, when to stop, and when to start," and she was the one who managed their financial affairs.

Paul believed the relationship between his parents was good, and he never saw any violence between them. However, his father was not so restrained when it came to the children: Paul said he grew up under a "reign of terror." He did not remember himself being struck, but he remembered a great deal of violence directed toward his older sister. He always gave his father a wide berth.

In his recollection, his mother was not very affectionate. "She never held me, and she never said she loved me." Her own father had left her family when she was very young. "Maybe she had it in for men. Anyway, I had always had this feeling—going back to my mother—of hating women almost subconsciously."

Another event of his adolescence contributed to this hate. When he was a teen-ager, he fell in love with a girl in his class in school. One day, after returning his affections for several weeks, she dropped him cold. "That really shook me up." He developed a pattern of going out with girls and jilting them "just like that," which he attributed to his first disappointment in love.

He married his first wife, Connie, a social worker, when he was twenty-one. He had met her through a correspondence when he was in the service overseas, anxious to receive mail, and a former girl friend had given Connie his name. On his return from the service, they met and dated for a while and had a sexual relationship. Guilty about having sex with her after she had a pregnancy scare,

78

he decided to marry her. "I don't think we had all the right reasons for marrying," he said.

Their relationship was built around her taking care of him. "I like to be around women I can dominate," Paul admitted. "I took advantage of the fact that she loved me, and I pushed her to the limit. I made her do a lot of things for me I wouldn't do now—run errands, get up from the table all the time to get me things."

He was not completely proud now of the way he had treated her then. "I would say things to put her down in front of other people. I think I did it because she was a stronger person than I was in a lot of ways, and I had an inferiority complex about it. She was a better worker. She would stick to things and finish them. She was better at relating to people, especially at parties. I was more the wallflower type."

His domination did not generally extend to physical violence: he was not the type to do that, he told us. He felt he was trained well from childhood not to be violent toward women. Also, Connie was taller and heavier than he was.

As the marriage went on, Paul and Connie had a continuing conflict over having children. They were getting older and wanted kids, but she was unable to conceive. Though they consulted doctors, she wouldn't do the things that the doctors recommended to increase her fertility: she refused to take pills and got embarrassed about the procedures. Then she wouldn't agree with him about adoption. This irked him very much.

In addition, after fifteen years of marriage, he was getting tired of being catered to all the time. "She was doing everything for me; it was just too much. I didn't know if I was capable of doing anything for myself." So, at age thirty-six, he began to think about getting out of the marriage: "It was a divorce looking for a reason to happen." For a while he waited for her to do something wrong, so he wouldn't be the one to break up the marriage. "Finally, I just said, 'This is it,' and I made a big announcement. I had some second thoughts about it later, but, being a stubborn person, I never would turn back on my decision."

Though they separated, they continued to see each other. They had sex together a few times and even went on trips together. The day before the divorce was to go through, Paul had serious second thoughts. He called Connie up that night and asked her not to do it. But it was too far along.

The night after the divorce went through, Paul called Connie around dinner time and asked her to come see him. He was angry with her for going through with the divorce; in fact, they were both angry about the terms of the settlement, and he remembers they argued. Although his recollections are somewhat dim, he also remembers indicating that he wanted to have sex with her, but she refused. He pushed her down on the kitchen floor and had sex with her anyway. She cried, and kept her legs crossed as long as she could, "much longer than she would have if she had been playing a game with me." He knew she was uncomfortable, especially since she had a bad back, but she did not struggle too forcefully, and eventually she gave in. Although she had said she didn't want to have sex, he noticed that she seemed to become lubricated during intercourse, which he took as a sign of arousal. Besides, "I guess I was angry with her. It was a way of getting even. She had gone through with it and I guess I blamed her, although it was really my own fault. I was angry at myself."

He found the act satisfying, but almost immediately after reaching climax he felt ashamed of himself. She complained to him that she had only been divorced for a day, and already she had had sex. After they got up off the floor, she stayed for another half an hour, long enough to have coffee together, and then she left. They never talked about the incident together, though they continued to have sex after their divorce, and they are still good friends today.

A couple of years later, he got married again, and eventually had three children by his second wife. But after five years of marriage, this wife decided that she had had enough and was divorcing him. His second wife was much more assertive than his first. There had been no violence in this relationship and no forced sex, he said. He thought his sexual relationship with both his first and second wives was quite good, but he told us he does enjoy an element of force in sexual relations.

"I have this feeling of satisfaction if I can have intercourse with them, especially if they aren't quite ready. I don't like to admit it, but I get this satisfaction from feeling some dominance—a man-over-woman thing. It's like an animal instinct."

Asked whether he considered what he did to his first wife a rape, he said, "No. I never raped a woman. I've always felt a woman could do a lot more than she did to resist."

Paul's story has some important similarities to those of Ross and Jack, but also some important differences. Like the previous two men, he was not a chronic batterer. Although he had the makings of a batterer, he had also internalized strong prohibitions against hitting women, and these appeared to work. He did not hit. Unfortunately, he had fewer internalized prohibitions against forcing sex.

Like Ross's marriage to Tania, Paul's marriage to Connie was characterized by his compulsive struggle to be dominant. He saw that she was the "stronger person . . . in a lot of ways," and that made him feel inadequate. To keep her in line, he would belittle her, order her around, and take advantage of her. Then Connie took matters into her own hands and went through with the divorce in spite of Paul. To punish her and put her in her place one last time, Paul forced her to have sex on his kitchen floor. "It was a way of getting even," he said.

Two things seemed to contribute to the ease with which Paul overcame Connie's resistance and accomplished his goal. One was that their whole relationship had been rooted in a tradition of his dominating her. Apparently she had the strength to brook his opposition by going through with the divorce, but in a face-to-face confrontation, the tradition won out. The other thing that made this rape easy for Paul was that the relationship was now over. Many of the marital rapes we heard about occurred when a couple were about to separate. The men at this point became furious at their wives for daring to break the bond, but they were also aware that they no longer had to live with repercussions of their acts. With the relationship over, what more had they to lose?

One aspect of Paul's account was different from that of Ross's or Jack's: Paul owned up to an ingrained hatred of women. We believe that many men in our society do hate women; but usually this feeling is so conventionalized and culturally approved that they do not recognize it for what it is. For Paul, however, it was salient enough that he noticed. He traced the history of his hatred back through high school and grade school to his mother, who he thought "had it in for men."

Perhaps this hatred of women made Paul somewhat different from the others. Ross and Jack both sought positions of dominance in their marriages. They resented their wives, one for trying to "control" him, the other for subjecting him to the burden of a family. But Paul's animosity was clearly part of a larger war, part of his hostility toward all women. One expression of this hostility was his thinly disguised preference for coercion as a mode of sexual interaction. Paul was retaliating against all women, not just his wife, and perhaps this made him more like some stranger-rapists than like Ross or Jack.

Paul did show fraternity with Ross and Jack in some of his typically male attitudes toward rape. Like them, for example, he held the standard belief that women really enjoy being forced, at least on some level. Since Connie started to lubricate in the course of the rape, he quickly stampeded to the conclusion that she must really have enjoyed it. She was saying one thing, but her body was saying another. He preferred to believe her body. This gave him a handy rationalization for his violent behavior and justified his use of force.

The other masculine stereotype Paul displayed is the belief that a woman who really wants to resist sex with a man can do so. He did not consider the possibility that she was genuinely afraid, or that she was paralyzed by the tradition of obedience he had encouraged in her from the start. She had probably never gotten "nasty" with him in her life, but if she had "really" resisted, he said, he would not have done it. With a convenient kind of moral sleight of hand, Paul put the onus of the rape on Connie's shoulders: she didn't resist strenuously enough, so either she wanted it, or else she got what she deserved.

Ross, Jack, and Paul provided some revealing testimony about husbands who rape and why they do. Obviously not moral monsters, they talked about their problems and their fears in ways that seemed quite human. They explained and justified their behavior with attitudes that are probably shared by large segments of the male population. They made a convincing case for how normal marital rape can be.

Researchers do not often ask men about this topic. The only other accounts by wife rapists that appear anywhere in the literature, as far as we know, are some interviews with incarcerated rapists[2] and some excerpts quoted by Shere Hite.[3] There is a prevailing belief that men will not talk readily about such events, or will give heavily biased versions if they do. Our interviews suggest this may not always be true.

Unfortunately, we cannot test the factual accuracy of Ross's, Jack's, or Paul's story. Perhaps they were much more brutal than they admitted. Perhaps they had raped more often than they claimed. According to their accounts, these men did not totally brutalize their wives the way some husbands who were described to us did. Rather, their crimes were force-only rapes. Nonetheless, these assaults were indications of a need to be in control, expectations that sex was a right and an entitlement, and hatred of women. These accounts, confirming much of what we have also heard from the wives we interviewed, contradict the image of marital rape as a marital tiff.

5

Marital Rape and Marital Sexuality

Sexual relations in marriage can be extremely coercive without a blow's ever being struck or a threat's ever being made. Women we interviewed talked about feeling forced to have sex with their husbands even when their husbands never lifted a finger. They talked about feeling that it was their duty, or feeling they had to do it to keep their husbands from becoming abusive. Some suffered terribly for years but always complied.

One woman said: "I wasn't abused by physical force. Rather, it was 'You're my wife. This is your duty.' That's how he made me feel. It felt like I had no choice. If I didn't comply I was afraid he might get angry, which might cause me to get hurt. But there was never any physical force. Just mental coercion."

Shere Hite quotes other women talking about the same issues:

"In my relationship I am forced to give sex because of the marriage vows. My husband has on occasion threatened to withhold money or favors—that is, permission of some sort or another—if I do not have sex with him. So I fake it. What the

84

hell. When the kids are older I just might lay my cards on the table."

"I really felt I was earning my room and board in bed for years, and if I wanted anything my husband was more likely to give it to me after sex. Now that I am self-supporting I don't have to play that game any more. What a relief!"

"My husband has a defensive personality. I have a horror of offending him. I always accommodate him, though it gives me no pleasure."[1]

In *Deliver Us from Love,* Suzanne Brogger puts it even more bluntly: "All the women who copulate to keep peace in the house are the victims of rape. All our grandmothers who just 'let it happen' were essentially force-fucked all their lives."[2] These women, all of whom have sex when they don't want to, feel different degrees of coercion. Some feel humiliated, prostituted, and angry at their husbands. Others feel less upset, like the woman who compared her sexual participation to "discharging an obligation like washing the dishes or doing the ironing." To her, sex was an unpleasant duty that was part of the bargain of being married.

Some feminists assert that sex as a marital chore constitutes coercion and a form of rape, since it stems from the unequal position of women who cannot afford to challenge their husbands. As Shere Hite says, "Anyone who is economically and legally dependent on another person, as women traditionally have been and in the majority of cases still are, is put in a vulnerable and precarious position when that person expects or demands sex or affection. . . . The fact that she does not feel free not to please him . . . reveals the presence of an element of fear and intimidation."[3]

But many women are reluctant to call such sexual intimidation rape. Oppressive though it may be, they feel that it involves a qualitatively different kind of coercion from rape and are aware of a certain voluntary submission on their own part to the obligation.

"I know I was feeling coerced and not doing it willingly most of the time," said one interviewee. "But in a way I'm not sure it was done by him. It was really my own upbringing and the things that I'd been taught. It came from me. He couldn't have really raped me. I was allowing my own body to be violated, and that's not rape. My allowing it is what makes it not rape."

Is it rape when a woman has sex to "keep the peace in the house"? On the one hand, calling it rape highlights how oppressive and coercive sex is under such circumstances. On the other hand, calling it rape means substantially expanding—and at the same time, diluting—the meaning of the word "rape."

We think there are some important distinctions to be made here. Women can be coerced, tricked, pressured, and bullied into having sex in a variety of ways, all of which are unpleasant and demeaning. These different kinds of coercion can be categorized into four basic types: social coercion; interpersonal coercion; threatened physical coercion; and physical coercion.

Social coercion is the pressure women feel as a result of social expectations or conventions. Many women believe they must have sex with their husbands because it is their duty, part of their role as wives. One woman says, "I'm not supposed to say no since I'm legally married." Another says, "With my husband I sometimes feel obligated because I'm his wife and, after all, he does pay for everything. . . ."

Adding to the pressure on women to meet these expectations is the awareness that others may judge them inadequate, frigid, or withholding if they don't. Society judges harshly women who refuse their husbands sex, considering them selfish and bad wives. For centuries, the Catholic church has taught that it is a sin for women to refuse their husbands sexual intimacy.[4] Wives were actually obliged to report such refusals in confession. The social pressures on women to have sex with their husbands even when they do not want to are strong and backed by tremendous authority.

Social coercion is institutionalized in the culture as laws, customs, and religion, and internalized by women in the course of growing up. It could be argued that all social expectations—such as those making us stop at stoplights or serve ice cream at the end rather than the beginning of the meal—are coercive. But social expectations that pressure people into behavior that is unpleasant and detrimental to their own dignity, autonomy, and self-interest are the ones that are coercive in the sense we are discussing here, and the pressure on women to have sex with their husbands when they do not want to fits this definition.

Interpersonal coercion occurs when a woman has sex with her husband in the face of threats that are *not* violent in nature. If she does not have sex with him, she feels that her husband will be angry with her, or she believes her husband will deprive her of money or help she needs. For example, some husbands have threatened to leave or to have affairs with other women if the wives don't comply. The women in Brogger's quote who "copulate to keep peace in the house" are the victims of interpersonal coercion. They have sex to avoid the implied threat of unpleasantness or conflict with their husbands.

When two parties are on more equal footing, threats of this sort (such as a union's threat to go on strike) amount to negotiations, with each party using threats—implicit or explicit—to gain concessions from the other. In negotiations, each party ends up doing something it doesn't like to get something it does.

But in many marriages, a woman's dependency and powerlessness undercut her bargaining position. If a husband threatens to withhold money to buy food for the children unless his wife has sex with him, and if she has nowhere else to get the money, she has little choice. If she has no skills with which to earn an independent living and he threatens to leave unless she has sex with him, she also has little choice.

Interpersonal coercion can be devastating and traumatic, even though no physical force is involved. Much depends on the nature of the threat. A woman who believes that she will not be able to survive if her husband leaves may suffer greatly from the anxiety.

The interpersonal threats that a husband uses to force his wife may also be overwhelming because of their persistence and their abusiveness. She may find them humiliating, psychologically debilitating, and shattering to her sense of self-confidence and self-esteem.

Moreover, even when threats are relatively minor and merely concern having to face a husband's anger or having to get some special favor, it is intrinsically unfair and demeaning to have to perform sexually in exchange for ordinary decent and respectful behavior. That many women are obliged to accept this bargain is a testimony to the small amount of power and resources they control in their marriages.

Threatened physical coercion can range from an explicit threat to kill a woman if she doesn't comply, to the implied threat that she could get hurt if she doesn't cooperate.

One interviewee said, "After he had been abusive to me for a few years . . . I was afraid not to have sex with him when he wanted. I remembered abuse from other times. When I had been hit or hurt, it had been because I had been bucking him in some way." We talked to women whose husbands had never actually used physical force to get them to have sex, but who were very frightened that their husbands would use it if they showed the slightest resistance. As one woman told us, "In my mind I was screaming, 'Get away from me. Get your hands off me and don't do those things.' But I wouldn't say anything, only to myself. It was awful. . . ." Almost all the women had been battered in situations that did not involve forced sex and had a good taste of their husbands' violence. They walked on eggshells to avoid more abuse, and abided by their husbands' sexual wishes.

The fourth category, *physical* coercion, involves a man physically subduing his wife or striking her to get her to comply. This is the kind of force most people think of when they hear the term "rape."

Though these four types of coercion are distinct, most women we spoke with described feeling coerced at a number of levels simultaneously. The woman who said, "In my relationship I am forced to give sex because of the marriage vows. My husband has on occasion threatened to withhold money or favors," was describing both social and interpersonal coercion. Another woman said, "If I didn't have sex with him he would be nasty for weeks, and I was afraid he might hit me," indicating that she felt a combination of interpersonal and threatened physical coercion.

Coercion other than physical is often difficult to diagnose. For example, some women live under extremely unequal and oppressive conditions, but they do not report feeling forced to have sex. Perhaps their sense of duty is so internalized that they are not at all in touch with any sense of unpleasantness connected to it. Though there may be coercion present here, without their awareness of it, it is difficult to tell. Does this constitute marital rape?

In a different context many women—and many men, too—report that at times they have sex when they do not want to, as a way of placating a partner. Not all these circumstances are forced; many are quite freely chosen. When two partners are on equal footing in a relationship, each is often giving in on some points, even doing something he or she doesn't really want to. A person does a favor as part of building the relationship and believes that it will be returned in some other way. There are other relationships, however, in which a woman's dependency puts her in the position of always giving in, always being the one to compromise. Unfortunately, to decide which is the case takes a great deal of knowledge about the dynamics of the marital relationship and the couple's history, perhaps even direct observation of their life together. To decide when interpersonal force is operating in a relationship can be a most complicated problem.

So, we decided for our purposes to limit the term "rape" to situations of *actual or threatened physical force*, although we readily acknowledge that other kinds of force can be frightening and traumatic. A woman whose husband tells her he is going to humiliate her publicly if she won't perform some sexual act, for instance, may be making a more fearsome and devastating threat than a man who threatens only to push himself on his wife. We would be prepared to call this kind of coercion forced sex, but not rape. We also recognize that other forms of interpersonal coercion (such as blackmail) *may* constitute rape. Our focus in this study, however, is more limited.

The idea that coercion might occur between husband and wife requires accepting the idea that wives are independent people with rights over their own bodies. Yet this notion of autonomy flies in the face of many of our society's cherished images of marital sexuality and the ideology of obligation. Under the ideology of obligation, husband and wife are melded together in a unitary bond. Sex is part of the sacred glue of this union. An implicit bargain exists by which wives make themselves sexually available to husbands in return for being supported.

For some people, this ideology makes the concept of rape or coercion in marriage unthinkable. "Sex goes along with being married. I just can't even think of there being rape in marriage," protested one college student we interviewed. "If two people truly love each other—how could anything be called rape?" another said.

If some undeniable coercion does occur, the ideology of obligation generally requires that it be seen as the wife's fault for not fulfilling her bargain to make herself sexually available. "The husband could be raping his wife when she uses sex as a tool for shutting him off," explained another student when asked for an account of marital rape.

A common presumption in the ideology of obligation is that if marital rape occurs, frigid wives are to blame. Men rape their wives because their wives have been withholding sex from them for a long time. "If she doesn't want sex for a long amount of time for no good reason—let the old man go for it," recommended one student.

These comments also reveal a reservoir of hostility that many men harbor for what they see as sexually uncooperative women. To withhold sex is seen as an insidious and vindictive weapon that women use against men. Discussions of marital rape often bring out this hostility.

Not only are "frigid" women seen as being the cause of marital rape; they are blamed for all kinds of other male misbehavior as well. Take, for example, what Ralph Slovenko, a law professor, wrote in an article on marital rape: "Society has an interest in tranquilizing the male at home. [William] Manchester in his book *Death of the President* points out that only after Marina Oswald had turned Lee Harvey Oswald down, only after she had made emphatically clear that she did not want him—only then did he reach for his gun."[5] Withholding women are not just considered responsible for their own rapes; they may be held responsible for great social and political catastrophes as well.

The notion of frigid, withholding women is an extremely value-laden, pejorative image. But even in its less pejorative form, the idea of sexually uninterested wives and frustrated, deprived husbands is fundamentally tied to popular conceptions of marital rape. Because this sexual conflict is thought to be virtually endemic to married life in America, it is the most frequently articulated explanation of why marital rape exists and why it might be widespread.

Part of the conception is that husbands desire sex a lot more than wives, and therefore that a state of sexual frustration is the common lot of the married man. Popular as this idea is, the evidence for it is not very compelling. It is true that studies going back to the 1930s show some greater degree of sexual interest among husbands than wives. But the differences are small. For example, one of the more recent of such studies, on a sample of couples in Cleveland, found that husbands desired sex 9.2 times per month, while wives preferred only 7.7 times per month, or about 16 percent less than their husbands.[6]

A 16-percent difference is rather small, given the stereotype. But most of the available studies also show that the gap tends to be *perceived* by husbands as larger than it really is. Thus, in the Cleveland study, husbands thought their wives only wanted sex 6.5 times per month, meaning they actually felt they were being deprived of sex 30 percent of the time they desired it.

Besides, the fact that on the *average* husbands want more sex than their wives does not mean that most husbands live in a state of chronic dissatisfaction. In fact, the majority of husbands in the surveys say that they are quite satisfied with their current frequency of sex.[7] However, there is a group of husbands who have an extremely high expectation of how much sex they should have—and since the group of high-expectation wives is much smaller, this tends to raise the whole average for men as compared with women.[8]

Moreover, there is evidence that the gap in preferred sexual frequency may be declining.[9] Between 1965 and 1970, for example, surveys found a 21-percent increase in frequency of intercourse reported by married women—an increase due in part to the use of contraceptive methods (birth-control pills, IUDs, and sterilization) allowing more freedom and less anxiety.[10] Some of the wives' reluctance to have sex in the past has probably stemmed from a fear of getting pregnant. Although the conflict over sexual frequency may play a role in some marital rapes, it is not an adequate explanation of marital rape.

As we indicated in Chapter 2, we certainly encountered many histories of marital rape in which women had not withheld sex and there was little evidence of any other conflict over sex whatsoever. In most of what we called battering rapes, we found that husbands assaulted wives who were otherwise sexually available to them. These husbands attacked their wives not to have sex when the wives had refused them, but to punish and humiliate women with whom they were angry.

Irene Frieze, in her 1980 study of battered women, also found that a substantial number of the marital-rape victims in her sample had no conflict over sexual frequency with their husbands.[11] Forty-five percent of Frieze's marital-rape victims denied that their husbands wanted sex too often. Thirty-five percent said they had not been inclined to refuse their husbands' advances. So it certainly seems fair to say that a large number of wives are raped in marriages where sexual "withholding" is not an issue.

But it is also accurate that in other marriages conflicts over sex do lead to sexual assaults. Some of the women in our study reported that their husbands wanted sex more frequently than they themselves did. Other husbands wanted to perform acts such as anal intercourse, which their wives disliked. But we cannot jump from the observation of a sexual conflict to the conclusion that these men are being deprived in an objective sense.

In popular images of rape, rapists were formerly men who could not get enough sex in the socially appropriate ways—from wives, girl friends, or masturbation—so they went out and raped. It was thought that when society liberalized pornography and prostitution and extramarital sex, making it easier for men to satisfy their sexual needs, the frequency of rape would be reduced—a prediction that turned out to be badly mistaken.

In the last ten years, evidence has been amassed to disprove the idea that men rape simply because they are deprived. Studies of convicted rapists show that many of them are married or have ongoing sexual relationships.[12] A study of unreported rapists, men on a college campus who admitted to having committed sexual assaults, found that these men in fact had *more* sexual outlets and sexual experience than their classmates.[13] However, the fact that they are not *objectively* deprived, compared with the norm, does not mean that some men do not *feel* deprived. The college-student rapists who had had higher than average levels of sexual experience also reported having higher than average levels of sexual expectations. They thought they should be having even more sex than they were, and as a result they *felt* sexually deprived. The key factor was not deprivation but larger than normal expectations.

This describes some marital rapists, too. In rapes that occur over sexual conflicts, husbands are not necessarily deprived of sex. Rather, they have extreme expectations about what their sexual rights and privileges ought to be. Several interviewees mentioned husbands who wanted to have sex two, three, and four times a day. Others mentioned husbands who believed they had a right to anal or oral intercourse even though their wives objected. Extreme sexual expectations are often coupled with other aggressive and hypermasculine attitudes. In particular, the men's need for power and control over their wives seems conducive to marital rape when sexual conflicts occur.

Yet the mention of marital rape conjures up associations with frigid wives, not hypersexual husbands. It is also interesting that when men are described as sexually deprived, the problem is assumed to be that women are withholding sex, not that men have unreasonable expectations. Unfortunately, our cultural images of frigid and withholding women seem to be much more readily prevalent than images of unreasonable and hypersexual men.

The tendency toward sexual compulsivity in men and the "muting of erotic impulsivity" in women, to use Dorothy Dinnerstein's phrase,[14] is one of the basic realities of relations between the sexes in our culture. Unfortunately, the subject has not been very extensively explored by social science. Our own understanding of the conflict favors an explanation based on the very different cultural values into which boys and girls are socialized.[15] The male tendency toward sexual compulsivity has to do with growing up in a culture where frequent sexual access to women is treated as an important (if not the most important) test of adequacy as men. As several observers have pointed out, for men there appears to be a closer connection between having a lot of sex and feeling like a competent member of their sex than is the case for women.[16]

Frequent sex takes on added significance for men because of other important symbolic meanings men invest in sex. Sex, for one thing, signifies power. When men feel anxious about their power or effectiveness in the world, they often try to compensate through sexual activity. Men who feel unsuccessful in their careers will often try to gain back their sense of accomplishment through sex.[17]

Men do not have so many vehicles for affectionate intimacy as do women: nonsexual physical contact is harder for men, and intimacy based on the sharing of personal feelings is less common. When men feel a need for closeness or dependency, one of the few permissible means to express it is through sex. Thus sex has to do double duty in the fulfillment of many other of a man's needs,[18] and men seem to overvalue genital sexuality because it is one of their few available ways of getting close to others.

Women, by contrast, are socialized into a very different orientation toward sex. As they grow up, sex becomes tinged with connotations of danger and badness. Through sex, women can tarnish their reputations and become pregnant. The dangers involved in sexuality are not merely cultural stigmas. It is rational for young women to approach sexual interactions with apprehension, for they are indeed at high risk to sexual assault and sexual coercion. Moreover, males do use sexuality to exploit and retaliate against women. Women cannot readily assume good faith in sexual encounters. Trust assumes a very important role in women's sexual orientation.[19] The female adolescent subculture tends to assign different symbolic values to sex, too. Genital activity does not form the basis of fantasy so much as romantic ideas of becoming a couple, being treated as a special person, and exchanging affection and tenderness. This configuration of sexual needs tends to lead to certain characteristic conflicts over sex between men and women. Generally, men tend to feel that their sexual relationships lack quantity, whereas women tend to feel that theirs are lacking in quality. Men think they should be having sex more often, women that their partners should be more considerate, more tender, more romantic in their approach. Men tend to feel that almost any time is appropriate for sex, but women are much more sensitive to context. A man may just want to close the door on the children and have intercourse; a woman may be too distracted by the concerns of the household or a recent conflict with her husband to turn her attention eagerly to sex.

Women tend to be extremely attuned to the emotional climate and degree of trust in a relationship, and find that it affects their sexual desire. Many men often want sex no matter what is going on. Women, by contrast, often say that tension, anger, or unresolved conflicts with their partners undermine their interest. Men feel like having sex in spite of or sometimes because of the conflict, often to re-establish intimacy. As one woman said, "For him sex was a way of making it better when things were bad. For me, sex was a way of celebrating when things were good."

Power differentials between men and women play an important part in marital sexuality, too. Because women have fewer resources and less authority in relationships with men, they tend to use judiciously what resources they have. Sex sometimes becomes a crucial resource for a woman, and one way that she can exert some leverage in an otherwise adverse power struggle.[20] When the level of trust declines in a marriage, both partners become more aware of what they are giving and what they are getting. Women's lack of other bargaining points may heighten their sense of sex as a resource that can be used to keep the balance from becoming even more lopsided.

Curiously, however, we think that the conflict between male compulsivity and female inhibition is not a major factor in the problem of marital rape. It may be involved to some extent, as a kind of cultural backdrop out of which the problem grows, but it is less directly related than people commonly think. A great many of the men who do feel some subjective sense of sexual deprivation do not force their wives. For the ones who do, something else besides sexual frustration is going on.

Rather than arising from a conflict over sexual receptivity, we think marital rape can be more directly traced to certain specific male beliefs: the belief that a man has a right to sex from his wife; or the belief that women enjoy force; or the belief that violence is an appropriate way for a husband to express his feelings or get his way. Marital rape is also more closely connected to a man's over-whelming need always to dominate his wife or to have her fulfill his every wish or to have her as his exclusive possession. These seem to us to be the attitudes and the motives out of which marital rapes more often grow, not out of an intense sexual need, although such a need may serve as an immediate trigger in some cases. The key, then, is power and control rather than sexual deprivation.

Nonetheless, the issue of deprivation is important, because when the subject of marital rape comes up, many men cannot help seeing it through this lens. Men who feel at all deprived of sex in their relationships with women feel threatened by the issue of marital rape, and the topic sparks their grievances. These men correctly perceive that the issue of marital rape is about women's sexual autonomy. They hear women saying they want the right to refuse. Even if these men have never had a moment's thought about forcing their wives to have sex, the issue puts them in touch with their sense of deprivation and they feel threatened.

Yet, when the woman's sexual participation is based on coercion and obligation, it cannot be optimally satisfying for the man, either. A man may obtain physical gratification in such a relationship, but his emotional satisfaction must be diminished. The lack of satisfaction may in turn add to the compulsive search for more sex, because the sex is not satisfying basic needs for closeness and confirmation.

However, men need to realize that, whatever the problem, coercion is not the answer. As time goes on, women are less and less willing to enter into marriage with the implicit assumption that they have a duty to perform. And it seems almost inevitable that men are going to be less and less able to enter into marriage with the traditional assumption that if they coerce their wives, it's no one else's business.

As women become more equal partners in marriage and men can no longer get their way by intimidation, they may have to try negotiation. Opening up sexuality to discussion will force men and women to talk about their sexual needs and expectations. They may then find out that they are less far apart than they think, and that the problems that interfere with their sex lives are resolvable. For example, to take one classic conflict, a man may find out that if he took the time to stimulate his wife adequately, she would be interested in sex more often. Communication may be the beginning of better, more mutual, and equal sex.

6

Resisting Marital Rape

Women are much more successful at resisting rape than is commonly realized. A National Crime Panel survey of thousands of women showed that women rebuff two nonmarital rapists for every one who succeeds.[1] Screaming, running away, and fighting back all seem to increase a woman's chances of avoiding rape. Also, the more resistance strategies a woman tries, the better her chances are.[2]

Still unresolved, however, is whether these resistance tactics also increase a woman's chances of getting hurt. Social scientists do not yet know enough about rapists to specify under what circumstances resistance is most likely to backfire. There is, however, a growing consensus among rape researchers that the dangers of resistance to rape have been exaggerated, and women are increasingly being counseled to defend themselves actively.

One of the goals for our study was to learn more about resistance to marital rape. Since women manage to thwart two out of three nonmarital sexual assaults, we presumed that wives must thwart a substantial number of marital assaults, too. We thought the successful resisters could provide important wisdom to other wives about effective tactics for deterring and escaping marital rape.

With this goal in mind, we recruited victims of attempted as well as completed sexual assaults into our study. "Has your partner ever used force or threat of force to *try* to have sex with you?" we asked in our screening question. We also raised the question of successful resistance with all our interviewees, asking whether there had ever been instances when their husbands had tried to force them but they had gotten away.

To our surprise, we heard remarkably few stories of successful resistance to marital rape. In spite of the phrasing of our recruitment question, only two of the volunteers were victims of merely *attempted* rape. The remainder had actually been raped. And to the question "Have you *ever* successfully resisted an instance of sexual assault by your husband?" only a minority of our interviewees—27 percent—replied "yes."

However, we think there was successful resistance to marital rape more often than we were being told. Resistance to sexual coercion in marriage is a subtle process, and we believe many of our respondents were not aware of practicing it, even when they were doing so effectively. The subtlety of the process goes to the heart of an important difference between marital rape and rape by someone with whom a woman is not on intimate terms: a spouse has to be substantially more forceful and brutal for a wife to consider herself in the middle of an assault.

An example illustrates the difference. Suppose a stranger approaches a woman on a city street, roughly grabs her breasts, and tries to kiss her. She shouts, "Get away from me," pushes him away, and runs for safety. This woman is likely to see herself as having resisted a serious sexual assault. She is also quite likely to remember the incident and report it if an interviewer inquires about instances of sexual assault.

When a husband seizes his wife, grabs her breasts, and tries to kiss her, she may react similarly and successfully repulse him. However, she is not likely to interpret the experience as a sexual assault that she has just thwarted. And since she is less likely to perceive it as a "close call," she will probably not bring the incident up when a researcher asks her whether she ever successfully resisted an assault by her husband. In marriage, less aggressive attempts at sexual coercion—which constitute many of the attempted sexual assaults—are less likely to be remembered; thus the successful resistance is likely to be minimized as well.

In general, the successful resistance that was recounted involved dramatic events. The assaults in question were substantial and the countermeasures, also substantial, were not easily forgotten.

One interviewee struggled valiantly, and remembered her victory and battle scars with a great deal of pride. Priscilla, a thirty-one-year-old woman, was divorcing her husband after fourteen years of marriage. On occasion he had been very violent and abusive to her, in one case threatening her with a pistol. After their separation he had returned on several occasions to harass her and try to get her to have sex with him. One time she got him to leave by threatening to throw boiling water on him. Another time, however, he arrived when she was sick in bed and feeling very vulnerable. He pulled the covers off, hiked up her nightgown, pulled down his own pants, and tried to climb on top of her. A serious scuffle ensued. She tore at his hair, pinched his nose, kicked him, and twisted and turned as he tried to force her legs apart. She was determined not to let him succeed. After about a half hour of this wrestling, he gave up disgusted. Priscilla is proud of her resistance, especially considering his enormous size and weight (6'5", 300 pounds). She believes her firm resolve was crucial. The following day she found he had dislocated her hip in the struggle.

Priscilla believed her success was in large part attributable to

101

her determination. She had made a prior decision that she was not going to give in, and she stuck with it. As Pauline Bart's research has shown, women who are most concerned about *not being raped* have a greater likelihood of fighting off a rapist than women who are most concerned about *not being hurt*.[3] Priscilla was clearly in the former category, even willing to suffer injury in her struggle. The fact that she was separated from her husband and was intent on a divorce may have also strengthened her resolve and her resistance.

Margaret, another of our interviewees, described a successful struggle that, like Priscilla's, bore many similarities to accounts of successful resistance in stranger-rape situations. Margaret was a forty-six-year-old woman whose first husband, a farmer, had been an alcoholic. After fifteen years of marriage, she had ceased to have any sexual desire for him and had decided to leave. One evening, as she went to leave the house to go to work, her husband pushed her down in the kitchen, got on top of her, and began to bang her head against the floor. Though she managed to get up and away, he refused to let her out the door. She went into the kitchen, got a knife, and lunged at him. When he moved away, she slipped out the door. Feeling it was the safest place to go, she went to work. The violence of this experience made her realize that she had to end her marriage as soon as possible. The next day she got a lawyer and filed for a divorce.

Introducing a weapon on the scene of a domestic struggle can be a risky maneuver. Margaret's husband, however, unlike many in our sample, was not an intimidating, hot-tempered man who might have wrenched away the knife and used it against her, but was a depressed and ineffectual person, and Margaret clearly felt she could control the situation. A similar move by some of our other interviewees might have ended in disaster.

For some of the women we spoke with, the most effective defensive measures were not physical resistance, but threats tendered with the conviction necessary to make them credible.

Isabel was a forty-three-year-old woman with a graduate degree who worked for a television station. There was not much violence in her marriage, but on two occasions her husband had come home drunk and sexually assaulted her. The first time she struggled to no avail. The second time he attacked her at three in the morning, while she was in bed. Since she was healing from a cervical biopsy, and afraid of injury, she did not struggle. However, the next morning, while her husband was still asleep, she went down to the kitchen and began to slam pots and pans together, making a tremendous commotion. When he came to see what was the matter, she told him forcefully that if he "ever, ever did it again," she would kill him. The forced sex never recurred.

Isabel made the boldest threat she could make. Although her husband may have wondered whether she really meant it, it obviously gave him pause. Many battered and sexually assaulted women say that they fantasize about killing their husbands, but it is our impression that few ever make such a threat to their husbands as a way of deterring the violence.[4] They doubt their own credibility and—perhaps justifiably—fear that such threats would lead to escalation of the abuse.

Isabel's threat to kill her husband, besides being delivered with conviction, was also made before a pattern of assault was allowed to build up. Jean Giles-Sims, a sociologist who has taken histories from many battered women, believes that some women can prevent further violence by taking decisive action at the first physical assault.[5] Unfortunately, many commonly try to ignore the first few incidents and restore life to the *status quo ante* as though nothing had happened, on the belief that the violence was an aberration and would not happen again. The effect, according to

Giles-Sims, is just the opposite: the return to normal acts to reinforce the violent behavior, because the husband now knows life
will still go on as usual when he does it. Both Giles-Sims and Murray Straus, another family-violence researcher, suggest that it is
crucial for wives to react quickly after a violent episode, making a
credible threat to leave or take other action should the violence
ever recur.[6] This is what Isabel did, and it worked.

Researchers from the University of Wisconsin have also been
interested in uncovering the kinds of personal strategies that
work to deter abusive husbands.[7] Through ads in the local papers
they recruited 136 women who said they had successfully "beaten
wife beating" (the research focused entirely on wife beating and
made no reference to marital rape). The researchers then talked
to the women about what kind of strategies had been most successful in ending the abuse.

Two active-resistance strategies turned out to work particularly
well for these women. One was making threats; the second was
defending themselves. The threats (all nonviolent) consisted primarily of threats to leave, get a divorce, or call the police. Interestingly, despite their efficacy, threats were among the least
utilized defense strategies, especially in early battering incidents:
only 10 percent made a threat to leave or call the police after the
first beating.

Moreover, "the women who were most successful with the
threatening technique were those who were able to convince their
husbands that their threats were serious, not frivolous. The husband had to believe that there was a high probability that his wife
would follow through on the threat if he did not end his abuse. For
this reason, the successful use of threatening was often combined
with the involvement of a formal help-source (such as an attorney)."[8] The research appears to support Giles-Sims's advice about
the need for early and credible threats to thwart the repetition of
abusive incidents.

Aggressive self-defense, the second strategy that the abused women recommended as an effective deterrent to abuse, involved a range of responses, including hitting, biting, and kicking. But such action also had a high and costly failure rate. Though 26 percent of the wives said aggressive self-defense resulted in a termination of the violence, 42 percent said that it made husbands angrier and intensified the abuse—a risky technique at best.

There were other strategies that the women employed. Some tried to talk their husbands out of their behavior, some to hide or avoid their husbands. Although the latter maneuver might postpone the abuse, it rarely ended the episode. Talking was also a relatively ineffectual technique, both for the short- and long-term protection of the women.

Unfortunately, for every woman in our sample who resisted successfully at some time, we have at least two whose resistance always failed. In many marriages, the tactics the women relied on would not work predictably: sometimes they successfully prevented a rape and sometimes not. No tactic worked for all the women.

Jessie, for example, struggled against her husband as valiantly as Priscilla, but was overpowered just the same.

Jessie was a twenty-two-year-old woman who worked as a manicurist. For a year and a half she lived with an underworld character who beat her virtually every day, and who used force to have sex with her, she estimates, twenty to twenty-five times over a four-month period. Once in a while she resisted, but never successfully. "There was nothing I could do. If he wanted it, he wanted it. I fought him. I hit him. I scratched him. I kept saying, 'No, no, I don't want you.' I resisted to the point where I was just crazy, and that was when he tied me up to get it."

Running away and hiding also ended in failure for several of our interviewees. One ran to the bathroom and locked the door; another ran into the bedroom and barricaded herself in. In both cases, their husbands broke down the door and raped them anyway.

Then there was Georgia, a twenty-two-year-old woman whose husband raped her on the second night of their marriage. She reported struggling for close to a half an hour before her husband overpowered her. Even when she vomited on both of them, he still didn't relent. In fact, this made him madder, and he started to punch her.

In many cases women did not try to resist, because they knew from experience that it was futile. About a quarter of the wives said they hardly resisted at all, or only occasionally.

But is it rape if a wife doesn't resist? Many people define rape more by the quality of the resistance than the quality of the attack; the absence of resistance makes them doubt that an assault has really taken place. In our society, ideas about violent encounters are dominated by male-oriented stereotypes concerning struggle and resistance. Conditioned by the rough-and-tumble fare of television and movies, many people have strong preconceptions about how someone is supposed to react when confronted by threat to life, limb, or valuable property.[9] A "man" defends his valuables. A "man" puts up a fight. A "man" resists, especially if no weapon is involved. Judged by these standards, the sometimes passive behavior of women in sexual assaults makes no sense. Since other attitudes already prime people to be suspicious of rape complaints, an absence of resistance feeds their skepticism about the seriousness of a rape. This skepticism takes the following forms:

- If she didn't clearly say no, then how can it be called an assault?
- If she didn't fight back, how do we know she really didn't want him to do it?
- If she didn't put up a struggle, she probably didn't really mind it that much.

- If it happened so easily, it couldn't possibly have been that traumatic.

Since we believe these are stereotypes that hamper people's understanding of rape victims, we talked at length to our interviewees about their immediate reactions to the assault. Were there other things they wished they had done? How did they perceive their options? Why did they react as they did?

One reason some women scarcely resisted was that the attack on them was so sudden, unexpected, and disorienting.

K ate, a thirty-two-year-old music teacher, described a single incident of forced sex by a boy friend, a very militant political activist with whom she had been living. The two of them had been staying in the country, trying out a back-to-the-land life style of housebuilding, weaving, and working on environmental politics. Their living together was not working out, and she had come to accept a break-up as inevitable. One night in bed they had a discussion about their relationship, and since it seemed to be leading nowhere, she rolled over to go to sleep. Suddenly he grabbed her and pinned her arms back with an angry roughness. He forced his mouth over her mouth, spread her legs apart, and raped her. She was so overwhelmed by the unexpected violence of it that she does not remember resisting except to ask, "Why are you doing this?"

Kate's story reminds us that in many relationships the possibility of assault is far from a woman's mind. Life in a marriage may go peacefully for years. Most of us trust in the comforting illusion that among family and intimates we are safe from attack. We have not considered the possibility of assault by an intimate, and so we have not rehearsed reactions. We deliver our vulnerable selves up to them in hundreds of ways every day. An unexpected sexual assault may provoke a flood of contradictory reactions—surprise, shock, anger, and fear. Before a woman has time to assimilate what is occurring, she may already have been overpowered. Kate made clear her lack of compliance when she confronted her boy friend with "Why are you doing this?," but otherwise her defenses were overwhelmed by the blitz.

Conversely, a second factor that inhibited resistance on the part of women we spoke to was the fact that many of their husbands had hurt them badly in the past. When sexual assaults began, their first instinct was to go limp to protect themselves as best they could.

Darlene, age thirty, was married to a man who abused her physically and sexually throughout twelve years of marriage. His violence toward her was more a matter of domination than of anger. He never drank and never hit her in a rage but, rather, in a cool, calculated way whenever she disobeyed him. He had bloodied her mouth, blackened her eyes, burned her with a cigarette, and once broken her ear drum. Sex was an everyday requirement, and if she balked he would throw her on the bed and say, "We're going to anyway." "I learned very early not to fight back," she said. Resistance was only a ticket to further and more violent abuse. "I'd just go along with the program. It was easier that way."

Another woman said, "When he attacked me, I was afraid that if I fought back or resisted, he'd hit back and break a few bones." We have already spoken of Isabel, whose husband attacked her when she was recuperating from a cervical biopsy. Afraid of aggravating her wound, she said, she submitted passively. However, all the other women who expressed to us fear of injury were in abusive relationships and had been badly hurt in the past. It was not that a battered wife would never resist—in fact, many battered wives did resist on occasion. But when they failed to resist, fear of injury was prominent among their concerns.

Another reason many women chose not to resist was that they knew from the start that it would be useless. They had been overpowered before and knew their husbands' temperaments. Even where the objective size difference was not great, some wives still perceived a great physical gulf between their husbands' strength and their own. "Part of not struggling was just a physical thing, because I wasn't strong and I didn't feel strong," said one woman. Usually, women are not well trained in physical combat and are not psychologically, let alone physically, prepared for such situations. As little girls they were taught not to fight. Their sense of helplessness against force was virtually complete.

Other women felt impotent not so much because they were outclassed physically, but because the whole history of their relationship had been one of domination by their husbands. Knowing that their husbands customarily got their way, these women were not able to reverse the whole tradition at that moment. Ursula's husband, for example, had for years bullied her into sexual activities she didn't like. When he approached her threateningly one night after a party, the pattern of subservience was too automatic to break. "I didn't want to have sex, but I knew that there was no way I was going to stop him. So I just let him do what he wanted," she said.

At least three interviewees mentioned the protection of their children as a prominent aspect of why they submitted passively to sexual coercion. For two of them it was a question of whether resistance on their part would frighten the children and alert them to the fact that Daddy was assaulting Mommy. "All I could think was that [my daughter] had been through enough. I didn't want her to see this, too. So I just withdrew from the scene mentally, as I had done in previous episodes of physical assault. I thought, 'He's not doing this to me. He's just doing this to my body.' " Another wife said, "I didn't want to scream bloody murder and cause all that uproar with the kids in the next room." A third woman was more concerned with the physical safety of her son. She had discovered that when she resisted her husband's sexual advances, he would take it out the next day on the boy, beating him for some minor infraction. This fear for the children is particularly salient where the children are in close proximity to the place where the assault is occurring.

Some women's goal was simply to get it over with as quickly as possible. They had found that resistance only prolonged the conflict and the hassle.

Teresa was thirty-eight and had recently separated from her husband after thirteen years of marriage. A surveyor, he was an alcoholic who had a temper, though it never really spilled over into violence against her. Their sex life was not good: she had a lot of guilt about sex, and he was a premature ejaculator. Many times when he would badger her for sex, she would just roll over and let him enter her from behind, as a way of complying without really being there.

On one occasion seven years into the marriage, he used more force than usual. This time he rolled her over, pinned her down with his hands, and forced himself into her. She remembers vaguely trying to get him to stop by complaining about what he was doing, but she did not resist or push him away with any conviction. Resisting seemed like a lot of trouble to her. She knew he would come very quickly and it would be all over, and this was much simpler for her than making an issue out of sex. Besides, she knew how to make him come even faster than usual, and having sex when she did not want it did not seem like such a big burden or indignity. "I ultimately consented rather than take the chance of getting beat up or whatever could have come. I was no match for him anyway. I figured, This is so stupid. Let's get it over with."

Teresa's approach worked for her. Since sex itself was a nuisance that had to be endured, the episode of forced sex was a rather minor incident, with no long-term repercussions for her.

Expressing a similar theme, some of the women we interviewed talked about submitting under coercion as a way of keeping the peace. They had a sense that if they resisted or fought back, they would have to deal with the fallout from their husbands' anger in other ways—surliness over breakfast, meanness toward the children, coldness toward them. Acquiescing to force was the price they felt they had to pay for a bit of civility and cooperation from their husbands.

Another common and insidious barrier to resisting husbands' attacks was that the women did not feel justified in doing so.

Angela was a twenty-one-year-old woman who described to us her three-year marriage to an extremely violent man. He had at one time threatened her with a knife, and had actually stabbed a friend of his. He was very demanding of sex, sometimes insisting on intercourse three times a day. Completely unsympathetic if she wasn't in the mood, he would hit her or throw her out of the house. "I felt that since I was married to him I was obligated," she said. "He had me brainwashed." Because she felt guilty and inadequate for shirking her marital responsibilities, Angela could not object or resist with any conviction when her husband came on with force.

Angela was not the only woman who felt brainwashed. Others spoke of believing that they were frigid, cold, unloving, incompetent, and unfaithful. Their husbands would accuse them of being these things repeatedly, and they had come to believe them. Social stereotypes, often with the help of their own upbringing, had primed them to agree that if there was sexual discomfort it must be their fault. Since they concluded that they were—as one woman put it—the "moral lepers," who were they to object to their husbands' sexual coercion? Wasn't it a justifiable expression of the men's frustration over their failures?

Even when there was little active brainwashing, other processes conspired to sap the conviction of these women that they had a right to resist. If their relationship was deteriorating, they often felt responsible. If their husbands were in a bad mood, they saw it as their fault. Women play the role of emotional man-

111

agers in relationships, and there was hardly a woman who did not feel some element of guilt and blame for their difficulties, even if such guilt was self-imposed. When confronted by aggressive husbands, self-blaming women did not feel confident in their position or justified in resisting. Courses on rape prevention sometimes counsel women to be ruthless—a knee to the testicles, a finger in the eye, a kick to the kneecap, a blow to the ear drum. Even in stranger-rape situations, however, women find it hard to use these tactics. Their lack of physical training makes it difficult, as does their socialization not to hurt others. Moreover, many have little confidence that they can use the technique effectively and they fear for the consequences if they fail.

Not surprisingly, we did not encounter any of these aggressive resistance techniques among our sample of sexually assaulted wives. The strongest tactics used were Priscilla's threat to pour boiling water on her husband and Margaret's wielding of a knife. But we also noticed that there was a reluctance, even among the most confident women, to use such strategies. Few women ran out of the house, or tried to summon help by screaming or telephoning. Few picked up objects with which to defend themselves.

When we asked women specifically about the use of the more effective resistance techniques, their answers gave us insight into some of the special problems of resistance to sexual assault in a marriage. These women frequently stressed the need to keep things civil and maintain the façade of a marriage. Unlike victims of assaults by strangers or even dates, these women had ongoing intimate relationships with their assailants. A victim of marital rape had to face her assailant the next morning over breakfast. She had to interact with his friends and relatives. She had to ask him for money to pay the electric bill or to repair the car. He was the father of her children. In many cases, women were deeply dependent upon their husbands, and some were still in love with them. Unless the wives had decided to terminate the relationship, they felt an intense need to preserve its underlying fabric even if their husbands may have been shredding it. This made them unwilling to try many of the ultimate resistance techniques. Not yet ready to call it quits, they were not yet willing to risk an unpardonable offense or destroy the façade of the relationship. Running to neighbors or friends or summoning the police were therefore equally difficult to do.

Although their record of effective resistance, as they reported it, was on the whole rather poor, there was one area in which our interviewees had more success. At least a half dozen of the women who had not been able to deter forced vaginal intercourse said that they *had* been able to thwart their husbands' efforts to have anal sex (and in one case oral sex) with them.

The sexual abuse most of these women were subjected to was continual and merciless. Their husbands seemed to have no regard for them whatsoever, and the women felt helpless either to resist or to flee. Yet they were able to resist successfully when their husbands tried to force sexual acts that they believed to be repugnant and deviant. What prompted this turnabout? What was different for these women about demands for anal and oral sex?

First of all, the victims felt more justification in resisting, even when forced. Ordinary sex they considered their duty, an obligation of marriage. As we described earlier, some women were not convinced that they were right in objecting to forced intercourse. On the other hand, in their view, anal and oral sex were *not* obligations of marriage. In fact, social taboos still prominent among many groups brand these as illegitimate, even illegal, acts, which wives may feel more conviction in resisting because they know they have some social support on their side.

By the same token, the taboo status of anal and oral sex may have undercut the husbands' conviction as well. When their wives showed some resistance, husbands may have been more reluctant simply to bulldoze on, as they were wont to do when their wives resisted intercourse.

When wives were successful in refusing oral and anal sex, it was not because their resistance tactics were so much more threatening but, rather, that their tactics were more adamant, more persistent, and more convincing. What this suggests is the importance of the normative climate around sex in marriage. At present, a woman's right to refuse and resist is not clear to many people. When the social climate clearly reflects that right, we may expect the amount of marital rape to decline.

A first step toward changing this normative climate is to raise the level of awareness about marital rape so that wives can view their forced-sex experiences as rape. Typically, this is not the case, and the majority of marital-rape victims do not label their assaults as rape. In Diana Russell's study, for instance, virtually all of the eighty-seven marital-rape victims saw themselves as having been sexually abused by their husbands. However, only six mentioned the abuse in answer to a direct question on rape. Russell comments, "Had we followed the woman's definitions, we would have obtained the erroneous information that rape in marriage is very rare, when, unfortunately, this is not the case."[10]

Irene Frieze found a similar reluctance: 6 percent of a neighborhood sample said they had been forced to have sex with their husbands, but only 3 percent called the experience rape.[11]

A woman's reluctance to identify her sexual-assault experience in marriage as rape is understandable. As we mentioned earlier, when the word "rape" is mentioned, most people think of stranger-rape—"walking down the street and having someone grab you," as one interviewee put it. The stranger-rape imagery so dominates our understanding of the word "rape" that sexual assaults by intimates often do not fit the picture. This is particularly true when the rapist is a spouse, because it has been a tenet of law and popular belief that a husband cannot rape his wife.

Perhaps just as important is the fact that the word "rape" has powerful connotations, suggesting a grievous violation, moral outrage, crime, punishment, police, and so forth. Many women do not want, or are not ready, to attach such connotations to their experience.

Consider, for example, a woman who is still living with the man who has sexually assaulted her. Applying the word "rape" means seeing her partner as a rapist, and acknowledging a gross violation. If the woman is still trying to salvage her relationship, or if she is still too afraid to leave, she cannot afford to label her assault as rape. To do so would imply that she should be taking some decisive action, perhaps even leave. She doesn't want to face the fact that she is living with a rapist, that she is making herself vulnerable to rape.

Even a woman who is not living with her assaulter may wish to minimize the seriousness of the sexual assault. It may be less painful to think of it as "not rape." This may help her avoid blaming herself for not getting out sooner, or may help her feel like less of a victim.

Carla was an interviewee who first replied to us, "No, it wasn't rape," and then corrected herself. After thinking over what made her change her mind, she said, "Even though I felt awful, I didn't think of it as so horrible, because it was my husband." When she was able to recognize that it had been a real trauma, the word "rape" seemed apt.

Coming to see a marital assault as rape can be a very liberating process for some women. Sometimes it is liberating because it legitimizes the sense of hurt and anger that a woman feels toward a husband who brutalized her, sometimes because it helps erase lingering feelings of guilt or blame in a woman. Once she labels it rape, she sees that a wrong has been done that she did not deserve.

Teresa was a woman who had such doubts. One night her husband had suddenly rolled her over, pinned her down, and forced her to have intercourse. But she wondered whether she had resisted enough. "There is such a fine line there because I ultimately consented rather than take the chance of getting beat up or whatever would have come. I finally gave in." But she came to see that what had happened was rape—"When you're telling a guy to stop and he doesn't stop, that's rape"—her point of view changed: she no longer saw it as her fault.

Coming to define an assault as a rape helps some women to take action to protect themselves. We have mentioned the story of Priscilla, whose estranged husband would come to her house, harass her, and try to get her to have sex with him. Her friends suggested she warn him that she would have him prosecuted for rape if he tried it again. She hadn't thought about it as rape before. Once she did, she warned him and he left her alone. Her new consciousness that what he was trying to do was rape gave her added conviction to deter his attempts.

The experiences of women like Priscilla and Teresa suggest how important it is for women to be able to label their assaults as rape or attempted rape. Until recently, however, the act of labeling was made difficult by the absence of the label itself. That is why it is so crucial for the concept of marital rape to gain some public exposure, so that women will be able to apply it to their own experience and use it to help transform their lives.

7

The Impact of Marital Rape

Being raped by their husbands unleashed powerful emotions in the women we interviewed. As one woman said, "It hurt. It wasn't fun at all and I was very mad. . . . I really hated that man—I could have shot him. He didn't care. I've never hated anybody like that. I hope no one else ever has to go through it. It's like a pit inside, it hurts so bad. You don't know how to crawl out of it. You don't know where to turn." The trauma these women experienced—both in the immediate aftermath and over the long term—had a special quality not shared even by victims of stranger-rape.

The women's feelings immediately after their rapes were sometimes so complex that they were difficult to categorize, but they tended to be of four main sorts: betrayal, anger, humiliation, and guilt. With the passage of time, some or all of these responses changed or waned. Yet, for most of the women the rape experiences continued to have an emotional impact years, even decades, later. Among the more common long-term effects were the inability to trust men, an aversion to intimacy and sex, and a lingering, acute fear of being assaulted again.

The first time it happened, many of the women could not believe that their husbands had raped them. Many felt an overwhelming sense of shock, followed by a profound sense of despondency. They could not believe that their husbands, who were supposed to have a special regard for them, could have done something so frightening, so humiliating, and so demeaning. Sophia, whose husband beat her as he raped her, describes the feelings of betrayal that followed her husband's first sexual assault: "My whole body was being abused. I feel if I'd been raped by a stranger, I could have dealt with it a whole lot better. . . . When a stranger does it, he doesn't know me, I don't know him. He's not doing it to me as a person, personally. With your husband, it becomes personal. You say, This man knows me. He knows my feelings. He knows me intimately, and then to do this to me—it's such a personal abuse. . . ."

Compounding the betrayal for many women was the realization that their husbands had no awareness of the effect of the brutal behavior. Georgia remembered crawling over to her side of the bed after being sexually assaulted by her husband the second night of their marriage. He had beaten her, leaving her with a black eye and bloodied face and nose. Then, to her amazement, he moved over toward her and wanted to put his arm around her in a caring way. It made her cringe. She felt hurt and betrayed. "I couldn't believe that someone who loved me could do that," she said.

Although betrayal was a common response, anger and hatred were even more common. Anger was the most vivid feeling recalled by more than a third of our interviewees. Many women expressed their hatred in terms of a desire to take revenge on their husbands for the pain and humiliation they had caused.

Rebecca, a sixty-year-old fine-arts teacher who contacted us when she read about our research, articulated feelings expressed by many of the women in the study.

While lying in bed with her husband one night, Rebecca broke the news to him that her doctor had warned her not to get pregnant again because it might be fatal to her. In reaction, her husband forced her to have sex immediately, although she did not have her diaphragm in. "He threw himself on me like a dog," she said. "It was a murder, an attempt at murder. He knew what he was doing. It wasn't that he was lost in passion. He knew that I had almost lost my life in the first pregnancy. I would have killed him if I could have. I hated and despised him. Nothing he did later could make up for that."

Many others expressed the same sentiments:

- "I resented the fact that he was getting his jollies and I was hating every second of it. There were times when I just could have murdered him cheerfully."
- "It made me hate him. . . . Once, I told him, if I wasn't afraid of going to jail I would kill you."
- "So, he says, 'You're my wife and you're gonna' . . . I just laid there thinking 'I hate him, I hate him, I hate him so much.'"

Although many of the women felt this fury, few actually expressed their anger or put their feelings into action. Often they knew that to do so would be futile or disastrous. One woman we talked with actually did take steps to kill her husband. Where she worked, a chemist had prepared an arsenic powder for a colleague to use on some neighborhood raccoons. She stole some of it one day and took it home to put in her husband's food, but then decided against using it for fear of going to jail.

An intense feeling of humiliation was another major response. For many women this took the form of feeling defiled or unclean. A quarter of our interviewees reported that they felt dirty and degraded in the aftermath of rape. Isabel, who headed straight for the shower immediately following her rape, elaborated: "I tried to wash it away, but you can't. I felt like a sexual garbage can."

The sense of degradation is not limited to feeling physically de-

119

filed. Several women spoke of feeling used. "I felt like a prostitute afterward," one said. Another felt the same way because she had given in to get relief from the violence: "I felt like a two-bit French whore. What I was engaged in was nothing but prostitution. I was buying another hour of peace and quiet—that was all it was."

The rape itself was only part of the humiliation that left these victims feeling dirty. Many had been subjected to an additional kind of sexual abuse in connection with the assaults: their whole sexuality had been denigrated, in so many words, by their abusers. Sophia's husband persistently called her a "no-good tramp" and a "whore." Katherine's husband blamed their sexual problems on her: "I felt like a robot, a sex machine for him. If I didn't enjoy it, it was because I was defective or frigid. It wasn't his fault." The physical and sexual attacks suffered by Darlene were sporadic, but the verbal degradation was unremitting. He called her an "imbecile," a "moron," an "idiot." He was disparaging about her body and berated her "lousy figure." He referred to her as "the stupid bitch." He "talked me into believing that I wasn't much good for anything," she confessed. "He gave me a lot of insecurities I never had before—about my body, my smell, everything. . . ."

The verbal deprecation these women endured was connected to their sexual violation. They developed very negative self-images and began to see their lack of sexual interest as a character defect rather than as a consequence of the abusive relationship. A number of the women subjected to forced sex felt degraded and dirty, but those who suffered constant verbal abuse also incorporated that into their self-concepts and began to feel "like dirt."

A fourth pattern we noted among some of the women we interviewed was their tendency to feel guilty and blame themselves for what happened. They would imagine that the assault was their fault—for not being a better wife, or for not trying harder to make the marriage work. However, not all the marital-rape victims blamed themselves; in fact, the self-blamers were in a minority.

Irene Frieze, who found a similar trend in her study, also reported that those who felt most guilty held the most traditional ideas about being a "good wife."[1] Those who blamed themselves were also, according to Frieze, those who put up with the abuse the longest and suffered the most marital rape.

Joyce, a forty-nine-year-old woman who had lived in the same rural town her whole life, suffered sexual abuse during the course of her marriage. Though the abuse was brutal and physically injurious to her, Joyce blamed herself. In the aftermath of the sexual assaults, she remembers, "I felt sorry for him because I couldn't give him what he wanted. I would cry, but not loud enough for the children to hear." She tried to talk to him, but he told her the problem was that she "wasn't much good" and that she was not "doing her wifely duty."

Twenty-five years passed before Joyce left. "In part, I was not willing to accept that I had failed. I felt partly to blame. After all, it takes two. If only I worked harder at it, I thought, I could save my marriage. Am I going to let something like sex destroy it, destroy us, take away what I had worked so hard for? I guess I felt I was his property. I was being supported by him, and he did have the right to do with me what he wanted, whatever it was."

There did come a point, though, when Joyce questioned that "right," and five years previous to our interview she had obtained a divorce. "Life is too short to waste on so much pain," she concluded.

For several of the marital-rape victims, physical reactions—particularly nausea and vomiting—joined the emotional turmoil in the rape's aftermath. Lynn, for example, remembers escaping to the bathroom immediately after her rape, locking the door, and throwing up. She felt ill, hot and feverish, as she lay on the cold tile floor, angry at herself for letting it happen. Other women had to take care of physical injuries that stemmed from the rape itself.

Black eyes, bloody noses, cigarette burns, broken bones, all these and more were described to us as injuries inflicted in the course of sexual assault.

Another physiological consequence of forced sex was damage to the genitals and rectum. Rough, forceful penetration without adequate lubrication caused varying degrees of injury, including vaginal soreness, swollen labia, and, in some instances, lacerations. We commented earlier that a third of the women reported forced anal sex. All of these women described some degree of physical injuries, ranging from soreness to hemorrhoids to torn muscles. Genital injuries were particularly painful for women who were just recovering from gynecological surgery or from childbirth. Women who were forced often were also especially vulnerable to physical harm.

The man Carol lived with expected her to have sex three or four times a day. She estimates that about 60 percent of the time he had to force her: "If I didn't do it, he'd beat my ass. He told me, 'Do it or you're dead.' It got to the point where I had to keep going to family planning to get medicine to put on me because he was forcing me. The doctor was telling me that I was having too much sex and that I should cut down."

Carol developed venereal warts and started to have great pain every time he forced her. When she went back to the family-planning agency, they instructed her to refrain from sex entirely for a while. She told the doctor that her partner wanted it often, but the doctor told her to try to explain it to him. She responded that it wouldn't work, that she had already tried. The doctor told her to try a little harder.

Marge Piercy, in "Rape Poem," speaks for rape victims: "There is no difference between being raped and being run over by a truck except that afterward men ask if you enjoyed it." There is a popular cultural stereotype that, while loath to admit it, women really obtain pleasure from being forced to have sex. The stereotype is promoted particularly in pornography. Books and movies often depict women reluctant to engage in sex who are overpowered and even brutalized by aggressive men. The women are eventually aroused, come to many climaxes, and become passionately attracted to the men who raped them.

This notion achieved some scientific dignity in the once-popular Freudian theories of female "masochism." These theories, first associated with Freud and later with his disciple Helene Deutsch, held that pleasure in forced sexual penetration was innate to the female character, due to the nature of the female genital apparatus.[2]

However, in recent years, the idea that rape victims take pleasure in the assaults they suffer has been thoroughly discredited. Research on rape victims has shown that they overwhelmingly experience fear, pain, humiliation, and disgust.[3] Even women who admit to having pleasurable fantasies about rape report that actual rape experiences are completely devastating and bear no resemblance to the fantasy.

Yet, because marital rape involves spouses, the question inevitably arises whether some women find marital rape pleasurable. Some people have suggested that what we call marital rape may not be perceived in entirely negative terms by the women we are describing as victims. People wonder, for example, whether some women, basically inhibited by moralistic upbringing, find they are able to abandon themselves to sexual pleasure only when they are coerced by their husbands. They also wonder whether some couples do not have a mutually satisfying sado-masochistic relationship: he enjoys inflicting pain and she enjoys receiving it. If this were the nature of a couple's sex life, would it be fair to call it marital rape?

To address the question of possible masochistic enjoyment in marital rape, we asked every woman toward the end of the interview, "When you were forced, was there ever a time that you enjoyed it?" Over 90 percent of the interviewees answered unambiguously, "No." Some were understandably indignant that we would even ask such a question. Nevertheless, there were four out of fifty women who answered a qualified yes to the question. We questioned those women further in order to understand precisely what they meant when they said there had been some pleasure.

First of all, none of them matched any of the stereotypes about masochistic sex. They were not sexually inhibited women who found that being coerced was a means to open up and enjoy sexual pleasure. Nor were they women who had developed a sadomasochistic script with their husbands, fulfilling a forbidden fantasy. In many ways, they were remarkably like the other marital-rape victims in the sample. When they had first been sexually assaulted, they had all been angry, hurt, disgusted, and dismayed. They felt degraded, humiliated, and betrayed by the sexual behavior of their husbands; this was not the kind of sexual relationship they wanted, and they resented it.

It was only after the assaults were repeated on many occasions that these women reported that they began to have certain episodes of pleasure. At least two of the women came to accept abusive treatment as part of their marriages, and came to believe that the assaults were inevitable. They did not know how to avoid or stop them, but they were not yet ready to leave the marriage or lay down an ultimatum. So they accommodated to this mishandling and decided to try to derive what pleasure they could from a situation they believed they could not change.

Rose was married to a man who seemed obsessed with sex. He appeared to need to be angry with her in order to enjoy sex. He would hold her in a tight restraint or tear off her clothes, all the while yelling at her. Though Rose disliked this intensely, she learned to adjust to it, and there were times when she did get some satisfaction from such sexual interactions and even had orgasms. However, she made clear that despite the physical responses, the experience was only marginally enjoyable.

Jessie, the manicurist, was coupled with a man she called a "snake in a hole," a generally violent type who led a life in the underworld of gambling and pimping. As we mentioned before, he beat and raped her repeatedly and she was never able to success-fully resist his attacks. At one point he tied her up to have sex with her. "It hurt. I was mad. But you have to accept some things or you're gonna get hurt worse. If I played with it enough I could get into it enough where it wouldn't hurt and it wouldn't be so bad."

It would be a mistake to describe what both these women were feeling as pleasure. They were not experiencing happy sexual en-counters. However, against the backdrop of abuse and mistreat-ment, which they had come to accept, they found they could sometimes derive some sexual stimulation and satisfaction. This was what one might call a practical adaptation to painful and dif-ficult circumstances.

A third woman's experience, however, was different. Through-out the course of Sharon's twenty-year marriage, there were in-termittent periods of conflict, anger, and forced sex. Sharon was furious over her husband's sexual assaults and often resisted so relentlessly that he would leave her alone. Although she was not trying to get turned on, she said that there were a few occasions when she was aroused in spite of him and in spite of herself. Those episodes upset her even more, however, because she was so angry with him.

This fact of involuntary arousal, even in the face of a very neg-ative experience, has been noted elsewhere in the sexual-assault literature. There are accounts of other victims of rape and sexual abuse who were sexually aroused, even achieving orgasm, in the midst of pain, fear, and unpleasantness.[4] The human sexual ap-paratus does appear to have some degree of autonomy from the mind, and this is a source of confusion, both to victims and to out-side observers of sexual assaults.

Nicholas Groth, for example, has pointed out that in sexual as-saults committed by men against other men, the assailants often compel the victims to ejaculate, through stimulation.[5] Such vic-tims (the same is true for some child victims of father-daughter incest) report feeling betrayed by their bodies.[6] These confused feelings—and the accompanying sense of alienation from their own bodies and own sexuality—often compound the trauma of the assault. The victims are left feeling some sense of complicity and self-betrayal.

It is important, however, to realize that the presence of some element of arousal does not make the experience any less of a rape. Even a wife who ended up deriving some pleasure after an initial sexual assault by her husband can be a rape victim. The key issue is *consent*. As long as she indicated that she did not want to have sex, and as long as he used force and coercion, then he has violated her will and her autonomy. This is the essence of rape.

In addition to the immediate trauma of marital rape, the victims we talked to reported serious long-term effects. Some were still experiencing them five or ten years after they had divorced their husbands. They talked about an inability to trust. They talked about lingering fear and emotional pain. They talked about terrifying flashbacks and nightmares. They talked about apprehensions about men and sexual dysfunctions—problems that kept them from having a social life, or that interfered with subsequent marriages.

The destruction of the ability to trust was the most common long-term effect of rape in marriage that our interviewees mentioned. Marital rape constituted for them not only a sexual assault, but a violation of trust and intimacy. The shock experienced by a woman who was sexually brutalized by the man she had loved and trusted above all others did not wane quickly. More than a third of our interviewees felt that their ability to trust and develop intimate relationships with men had been impaired, the impairment ranging from wanting to withdraw from contact with men altogether to feeling great caution in relations with men; from an underlying disdain to an outright hatred. The impact for Ina, for example, was a lingering distrust about certain kinds of men.

Ina was raped and battered by her husband, a college professor.

She talked of the sexual abuse as worse than the intermittent violence, because "it was a constant thing." Ina felt that her experience had a lasting effect on how she related to men. "I know I'm not attracted to any men who are big. All the men I've dated since my divorce have been tall and slender or short and slender, small-boned. I also have to feel that a man is extremely gentle or I don't want anything to do with him . . . and I still sometimes get afraid when I'm alone with a man in his bedroom or his apartment." Ina's distrust focused primarily on big men, and she was proceeding with care. But for Harriet, and many others, the distrust went beyond extra caution.

Harriet was the victim of two force-only rapes near the end of her marriage. For three or four years after the end of that twenty-one-year relationship, Harriet felt the effects of the sexual abuse. She was not fearful of her ex-husband—"The spite I felt for him by this time was so obvious, I don't think he would have dared come near me again"—but she had harsh feelings for men in general. "For a good long time I got very turned off of men. I was untrusting. I felt a complete disrespect. I lived in a self-imposed exile." Harriet felt that in recent months she had started to come out of her shell and relate a bit better to men. But other women were not at that point yet.

Shirley, who stayed with her husband for years on the advice of her fundamentalist pastor, was getting her life together. After her divorce, she had gotten her high-school-equivalency diploma and started taking courses at a local college. Meanwhile, though the fear was subsiding, the scars were still there. "I really have a hard time relating to men," she said. "I don't trust them. I hope some day I will, but right now I'm very anti-man." Maureen, whose husband forced her to have sex several times and even crammed their marriage license down her throat on one occasion, echoed this sentiment. "I've decided no man will ever do that to me again. I guess I've got a mean streak in me toward men right now. I hate them."

The marital rapes created some very confused feelings in

women about men and intimacy. Cindy expressed this confusion in her discussion of love. She could not understand what kept bringing her back to her husband after beatings, forced sex, and even gang rape. "I really don't know why," she said. "I think it was because I knew how sick he was and how badly he needed me. I've always felt like someone when I felt I was needed. Maybe it was to punish myself, too. Even though I knew the kind of love he was giving me was wrong, at least it was something. It was better than nothing. So it kept bringing me back to him."

As a result of her abuse, she said, "I've had a very hard time trusting men. . . . I can't say I hate guys. I have the right reasons to, I know. I think Jimmy ruined it, so that it is going to take a long time before I can hold down a relationship with a guy."

Cindy's reactions illustrate how women's notions of love can be linked to putting up with extended violence. The severe abuse is seen as a sign that their partners are sick. The more serious the sickness, the more women feel that they must nurture and try to heal—even at the expense of their own well-being. When women like Cindy finally bring themselves to leave this kind of abusive situation, they often fear intimate involvement in the future. The experience of being raped or beaten by a husband causes many women to doubt their judgment about men.

Kate, the music teacher, had high hopes when she began living with a "new man," who was an environmentalist. But she left him in a matter of weeks, after one forced-sex incident. Compared with the other women in our study, she got out relatively un-scathed. Nevertheless, she felt the experience still affected her years later. She was not confident of her own judgment, because, she said, "I thought so highly of him and he turned out to be a rapist."

Terry, a victim of a force-only rape, also felt that the longest-lasting effect of her experience was on how she evaluated people. It represented a loss of innocence. "I clearly knew I was not going to get into that kind of situation again. I looked for people who would not do those kinds of things," she said. Jessie, too, felt that she was a much better judge of character now: "I'll never do it again because those traits are very easy to pick up." She explained that men like that are "snappy, or very quiet and uptight. They keep everything to themselves and then all of a sudden they'll just let it go. Take someone out for an evening and get them drunk and you'll find out a lot about these people," she added. "Bars are the worst place you can pick someone up, but sometimes they're the best because then you know what you're dealing with."

Many of the women we interviewed told us that when they later tried to establish relationships with men, they had sexual difficulties that they attributed to being raped by their husbands. Gail, at the age of twenty-one, was looking back over a terrifying marriage that had produced two children. When her suicide attempt failed to end the abuse, she divorced her husband, but hadn't "rid myself of the scars. He ruined my life," she said. "Until this day, I hate sex. I don't get nothing out of it. I hate it so bad. It seems like every time I have it, it's just a flashback."

Gail's severe and deep-seated abhorrence for sex was an extreme example, perhaps because what had happened to her was also extreme. She had been sexually abused as a young girl, in her mother's presence, by one of her mother's boy friends. That experience was followed by a pregnancy at sixteen and forced sex at the hands of her husband. Gail has never known a positive sexual relationship.

For Lynn, withdrawal from men was a reaction to years of sexual violence. Her husband used to control her by using her ponytail as reins to force her to submit, and shortly after her divorce she had her long hair cut off. Lynn has not let much time pass between haircuts since then. For a time, too, she wore clothes several sizes too large, for fear of being sexually attractive to men. Years passed and her aversion to sex has subsided, but she is still very sensitive to any false move. "A brief flashback can still ruin sex."

Gretchen was still struggling for a good sexual relationship more than twenty years after the end of her first marriage. Hospitalized years ago after her first husband ripped open her vagina with his fist, she has finally gotten over the nightmares. However, her two subsequent marriages have been plagued with sexual difficulties. Sex with her second husband was unpleasant, and it wasn't until she met her third husband that she began to enjoy it. Even now, though, there are things he can do to "shut me off like a faucet." Even if she is quite aroused and close to orgasm, she can instantly get frightened and "turn off" if he "pushes the wrong way or moves funny."

"My first husband hurt me so bad that even when my new husband hurts me by accident, it's just something my whole body reacts to, even though I don't want to."

Sophia's experience, like Gretchen's, has left her with persistent sexual inhibitions: she, more clearly than any of our other interviewees, felt she could have coped much better had she been raped by a stranger. A victim of many battering rapes, she had been remarried for fifteen years, but felt that her new relationship had suffered because of her inability to be "a fully sexual woman." Just recently, she had a hysterectomy, which seemed to precipitate additional sexual problems. She believed that it brought to the surface all the sexual pain she had felt years ago as a result of being sexually assaulted and never sharing it with anyone. She suddenly didn't want her husband to be physically close. "I felt a suffocating sensation when he tried to put his arms around me."

It is recognized that fearfulness is one of the long-term effects of stranger-rape. In its aftermath, victims often report not wanting to be alone, not wanting to go out in public, having nightmares and anxieties that the rapist will return to retaliate. Fearfulness is also a common long-term effect of marital rape, particularly of the battering and obsessive rapes. Even though most of the women we spoke with had ended their marriages, their fear of their husbands had by no means ceased. Often it was very deeply ingrained, and generalized to other men. Some of the marital-rape victims had lived in terror for years, never knowing when a physical or sexual assault might come. This insecurity became almost instinctual and lingered even when the husband was no longer physically present, for it was hard to get away from the psychological presence of a brutal husband. Reminders of him were everywhere—in the furniture that they once shared, in the friends and relatives who knew him, even in the children who shared his features and still considered him daddy. When a woman was afraid of her former husband's capricious violence, it was hard to shake the feeling that he might reappear. Even when he didn't, the fear often persisted.

Christina had fled halfway across the country to get away from the partner who raped her, but distance did not assuage her panic that he was coming to get her. She had lived in terror for six months with a man who would beat her daily and routinely follow the beatings with sex. He had threatened to kill her if she ever tried to leave him. One day during her lunch period at work, she took eight hundred dollars out of their joint bank account, bought a plane ticket, and flew two thousand miles to a state she had never been to before. There, under an alias, "with not a friend in the world," she lived and worked for a year until she got up the courage to contact her parents and let them know where she was.

During that whole year, she lived "in a continual state of fear." Every now and then, she thought she had caught sight of her boy friend's car. More than once, she turned and fled down the street. For three years afterward, she was unable to have an orgasm. Violence and fear, she reported, were always on her mind.

For Susan, even the finality of divorce did not spell relief from her husband's violent assaults. Once he attacked her new boy friend, and another time spread paint remover all over her car. She still lived in fear of him, although she had not seen him in two years.

Intense fear plagued Gretchen for years. Though she moved to another country and remarried, she could not shake the terrifying idea that her husband was coming back to get her. It was not until eighteen years after she left that the nightmares of his trying to kill her finally subsided.

The symptoms reported by marital-rape victims bear some resemblance to those reported by hostages and other victims of terrorism.[7] Hostages report nightmares and lingering fears of danger from their captors, even when those fears have no basis in reality. They also suffer from recriminations, feeling that they must have been to blame in some way, that they were too cooperative, or that they were in some way guilty themselves. Indeed, the parallel between the emotional aftermath for hostages and for marital-rape victims is hardly surprising, since many victims of marital rape are in a real sense hostage to their rapists: they believe they are dependent on their husbands/captors for their survival, and they believe there is no escape.

Wives themselves are not the only victims of marital rape. Sometimes there are children involved, too. At least three of our interviewees were certain that conception occurred as a result of a forced-sex episode. Maureen, who was raped by her husband after they had separated, did not discover her pregnancy until the divorce was imminent. "I had to get an abortion," she said, which caused her great turmoil. "It made me hate him even more."

The two other women bore the children conceived in marital rape. Both, interestingly enough, were talked out of getting abortions by doctors to whom they turned for help. As a result, each ended up with a child she did not want, a child whose very existence reminded her of a painful experience. The devastating effect on the child was described by Rebecca. She was the interviewee whose husband forced himself on her when she informed him that the doctor had told her it would be unsafe to have any more children, and she became pregnant as a consequence of the forced sex. Her first impulse was to have an abortion, but that was no easy matter. The same doctor who had warned her against having children now encouraged her to go ahead. Another doctor told her that if she had an abortion, she would feel guilty for the rest of her life. "I was intimidated and horrified by that thought," she recalls.

She had the baby and almost died, losing eleven pints of blood and going into shock during childbirth. Her recovery made the front page of her local newspaper; ironically, the spotlight went to her husband, who had donated blood to help save her.

The baby boy was not wanted. "It was an entrapment beyond description," she explained. "The child was cursed from birth." He ended up with severe emotional problems and was eventually removed from the family by child-protection workers concerned about his mental health.

Other children are affected by marital rape not because they are the products of the rape, but because they are witnesses to it. A quarter of our interviewees said they had been raped in the presence of others, most often their own children. Psychoanalytically oriented psychiatrists, starting with Freud, have warned against allowing children to view the "primal scene." They reported cases that they believed showed that some long-lasting disorders started with children's fright over seeing their parents having intercourse. Some modern commentators have made light of the early, Freudian preoccupation with the "primal scene." They point out that in many of the world's cultures, adults sleep in the same room, so children inevitably witness parental intercourse without necessarily incurring any ill effects.[8] But maybe the Freudians did stumble upon an important phenomenon. What concerned Freudians specifically about the primal scene was that the young children would "misinterpret" the intercourse as an act of aggression. The children thought that Daddy was hurting Mommy; this alarmed and frightened them, and gave them a particularly fearful notion of sex.[9]

Is it possible that children traumatized by the "primal scene" were not just witnessing loving intercourse but viewing marital rape? Perhaps the children were not misinterpreting the acts they witnessed, but had perceived the emotional content of the scene quite correctly. It is altogether plausible that children exposed to marital rape may, in fact, suffer the kinds of long-term effects that psychiatrists have ascribed to the viewing of the "primal scene." Perhaps the point is not that parental sexuality is traumatizing to a child, but that parental violence is.

Though the women we interviewed reported a wide variety of long-lasting effects from the abusive marriages they endured, it was not always easy to allocate responsibility for the effects. These women had generally been through a great deal of suffering. Some were battered in addition to being raped; some had been sexually abused as a child besides being sexually abused as a wife; most had been psychologically abused, denigrated, and berated; almost all had gone through the traumatic experience of a broken marriage.

We were faced with the difficult task of determining whether the long-term effects they had suffered were attributable to the marital rape itself, or to the other abuse. The evidence we relied upon was their own assessments and perceptions: we asked many of the women who had also been battered to compare the effects of the marital rape with the effects of other abuse. All but three of the women reported that the sexual assaults were more devastating.

Lynn endured years of physical and sexual violence before she gave up. Looking back on the marriage, Lynn feels that the sexual abuse was the worst part. "The violence felt like it was external. But the sex, the sex was taken from me."

Ina, the wife of the college professor, was also more traumatized by the sexual abuse. "The physical stuff was over in a couple of hours," she said, "but the sex was a constant thing."

134

Sophia, too, recalls the acute aftereffects of the marital rape as the most devastating thing. "The physical abuse was horrible, but that was something I could get over. It was like a sore that heals. When he forced me to have sex with him, that was more than just physical. It went all the way down to my soul. He abused every part of me—my soul, my feelings, my mind. . . . It was just as much a mental rape as a physical rape, and I don't think that there is anything worse than that."

There are at least two important factors at work that make marital rapes seem particularly traumatizing in the long run compared with beatings. Beatings seem more external, and the physical injuries they cause soon disappear. But wives who are raped often comment on the more personal, intimate nature of the sexual abuse: the psychic wounds it left felt deeper.

A second reason that the rapes seemed worse was that the marital-rape victim, more so than the battered wife or stranger-rape victim, had great difficulty sharing her pain with anyone. She was not asked about it, not even by doctors or police, and found it hard to bring it up in a context where she *would* talk about her physical abuse. "It's just easier to talk about being hit; it's not as humiliating," explained one woman. The fact that the trauma of the rape was not discussed allowed it to linger unresolved. This certainly added to its destructive long-term effect.

Shirley, however, felt that though the forced sex was degrading, it was not worse than the brutal physical violence she suffered. Shirley stayed in her violent marriage for years on the advice of her fundamentalist minister, who admonished her to "work harder" at it. The most awful part of the marriage for her was "getting my head pounded into the wall." That particular assault left her hospitalized with a five-day coma and a miscarriage.

For Cindy, too, the beatings and the forced sex were both awful, but she remembered the beatings as the worst part. Though she experienced repercussions from the coercive sex, she suffered that alone. Many of her worst beatings took place in front of her six- and seven-year-old children. She was most traumatized by the fear that they would always remember it and continued to worry about how they were affected. For women like Shirley and Cindy, there was some traumatic feature of their overall abuse that stood out more than the forced sex. It was not that they felt unaffected by the sexual violence. Given their experiences, however, involving critical injuries, psychological terror, and the traumatization of children, their sense that the rapes were not the worst of it is not surprising.

The question of the relative effects of marital rape compared with beatings has also interested other researchers. To disentangle the effects of battering versus those of marital rape, Nancy Shields and Christine Hanneke, two investigators in St. Louis, studied a group of ninety-two women who were married to violent men.[10] They devised a way to control statistically for the severity of the battering a woman had received, and when they did so they found that marital rape had special long-term effects that were separable from the beatings. Marital rape by itself, they concluded, was especially damaging to a woman's self-esteem: women who had been raped felt worse about themselves than women who had only been beaten. Marital rape also had an especially corrosive effect on a woman's attitude toward men in general—more than was reported by the victims of beatings alone. Shields and Hanneke also found that the more *often* a woman had been raped by her husband, the more severe the long-term effects were likely to be, particularly in the area of self-esteem. Women who had been raped frequently were also more likely to have psychosomatic symptoms resulting from their abuse, and to make suicide attempts.

Disregarding such results and the testimony of marital-rape victims, many public figures callously dismiss the trauma of marital rape. In their minds, the injury of such rape is diminished because of the relationship between rapist and victim.

Charles Burt, defense attorney for marital-rape defendant John Rideout, made this point in blunt terms. "This isn't like he's grabbing some lady off the street," Burt complained. "This is a woman he may have made love to hundreds of times before."[11]

Writing on rape in marriage for the hundreds of thousands of readers of the Sunday magazine supplement *Parade,* Lloyd Shearer made a similar comparison: "Many U.S. jurists agree that when a husband compels his wife to engage in sex relations, she suffers relatively little of the psychological trauma incurred in rape by a stranger."[12]

Finally, in his 1981 statement at hearings by the Senate Judiciary Committee, Alabama Senator Jeremiah Denton was also confident that forced sex in marriage was less serious than rape by a stranger: "The issue is whether the . . . drastic punishments for rape should apply. The answer depends on whether the anguish caused by intercourse forced by a husband is equivalent to that inflicted by intercourse forced by someone else. . . . The character of the voluntary association of a husband and wife . . . could be thought to mitigate the nature of the harm resulting from the unwanted intercourse."[13]

The facts about marital rape belie the assumptions of such arguments. For example, Diana Russell, in her survey of San Francisco women, found that more of the marital-rape victims reported great long-term effects than victims of any other kind of rape.[14] Fifty-two percent of the women raped by their husbands or ex-husbands said the long-term effects had been great, as against only 39 percent of the victims of stranger-rape. Pauline Bart, in her report on over a thousand rape victims who answered a questionnaire for *Viva* magazine, found that more women raped by husbands became sexually dysfunctional than those raped by dates or strangers.[15] What commentators like Shearer and Burt and Denton seem to misunderstand are the unique elements of marital rape that can make it potentially so traumatic.

Marital rape victims suffer from many of the same traumas as victims of other rape—the humiliation, the physical injuries, the guilt and self-reproach. But they suffer some special traumas, too—betrayal, entrapment, and isolation. They have been violated by someone they loved. Many have been subjected to on-going abuse, sometimes as virtual hostages in their own homes. And they have no one to commiserate with in their pain. It is these special traumas that we need to acknowledge and understand in their full and terrible reality. When you are raped by a stranger you have to live with a frightening memory. When you are raped by your husband, you have to live with your rapist.

8

Marital Rape and the Law:
State Statutes and Public Opinion

Although it is true in most of the United States that a husband cannot be prosecuted for raping his wife, this exemption is given reality by a complex tangle of criminal statutes that vary from state to state with no obvious rhyme or reason. The statutes do all share a heritage in the doctrine inherited from the British in the often cited argument of Matthew Hale, but they have undergone variegated histories of revision and recodification in individual American states. For example, a conservative farm state like Nebraska completely struck out its marital-rape exemption as early as 1976, whereas Michigan, a state that has implemented much progressive rape-reform legislation, still retains it. The pattern of state laws does not lend itself to easy explanation. Until the recent advent of lobbying efforts by women's groups, the pattern seemed to have more to do with quirks of the legislative process (a sympathetic contact on a legislative committee; a hurried vote in the waning days of a session) than any particular underlying sociological or political factor.

Moreover, the legal situation is in flux. Especially now, as the

139

problem of marital rape has gained the attention of women's political-action groups, the roster of state statutes is changing annually. In 1983, Kansas, North Dakota, Washington, and Wyoming joined the list of states that criminalized marital rape for cohabiting husbands. In 1984, New York and Pennsylvania were also added.

The major task of sifting through these changing state laws and keeping up to date on them has been undertaken by Joanne Schulman of the National Center on Women and Family Law with the help of Laura X of the National Clearinghouse on Marital Rape. Schulman has made a careful reading of the sometimes contradictory laws in each of the states and keeps a growing network of people informed about the current status of legislative action and court decisions. The overview of the national situation provided here relies heavily on her work.[1]

As of January 1985, approximately twenty-seven states exempted husbands from prosecution for the rape of a wife *with whom he is currently living.* (We say "approximately" because some laws are in transition, some are vague and have not been subjected to judicial interpretation, and in some states contradictory implications can be drawn from different statutes.) On the other hand, twenty states have in one way or another abolished the exemption and permit the prosecution of husbands who rape their wives under all or most circumstances. That leaves three states and the District of Columbia that have no explicit marital-rape exemption but in which the "common law" may be in effect; the existence of a true marital-rape exemption in these states is uncertain and needs to be clarified by the courts or the state legislatures.[2]

Though this tally is rapidly changing, the basic types of legal situations that exist in different states remain the same: the absolute exemption, partial exemptions, no exemptions, and "silent" states.

The most definite of the laws—the absolute exemption—are

those that give a husband immunity from prosecution until the moment when a divorce decree legally ends the marriage. In the four states that had such laws in January 1985 (Alabama, Illinois, South Dakota, and Vermont) an estranged husband and wife can be separated for years, and the wife can have made very clear by public actions (such as filing for a divorce) that she no longer wishes to be married to this man, yet she is completely unprotected by the law from rape. If her husband breaks in and rapes her the day before the divorce becomes final, he is as immune from prosecution for rape as is the cohabiting husband of twenty unbroken years. Even the existence of a restraining order against the husband does not nullify the exemption.

The particular injustice of such an absolute exemption from prosecution for marital rape is that a wife has no way of quickly and unilaterally getting protection. She must wait for the slow grinding of the divorce process and suffer vulnerability during a period that can run into months or years. Nor is this vulnerability a mere academic concern. As mentioned earlier, our research has shown that an important number of marital rapes occur during the separation period. This is the time when a husband is feeling the greatest anger and resentment, and when, in an impulse to retaliate, he may muscle his way into his wife's home and sexually assault her. Thus, laws that bar prosecution until the moment of divorce not only deprive women of an important right of self-determination—the right to withdraw sexual consent—but also endanger women by giving what amounts to a green light to embittered husbands.

Recognizing the special situation of separated and divorcing women, some states have put limitations on the spousal exemption. These limitations usually allow for the prosecution of husbands once the marriage has reached some legal "point of no return." These laws, which we call partial exemptions, appear to be based on the idea that the so-called permanent consent to sex granted by wedlock can be terminated short of divorce if a woman signifies by certain official actions that she no longer wishes to remain married.

Some of the limitations to the exemption are more favorable to wives than others, depending on how much "official action" they require of a woman before granting her protection. The least favorable limitation entitles a woman to protection only after the couple is separated *under a court order*. As of January 1985, the laws of eight states held this requirement: Kentucky, Louisiana, Maryland, Missouri, North Carolina, Rhode Island, South Carolina, and Utah. Of course, here, as in the states with absolute exemptions, a woman is to a large extent at the mercy of bureaucratic procedure. A court-ordered separation can take as long as a divorce and requires money for attorneys and court costs.

Certain other states limit the exemption a bit more strictly by mandating its end when the woman is living apart and *files a petition* for a divorce, separation, or annulment from her husband. In these states (Indiana, Michigan, Nevada, Ohio, and Tennessee), the woman does not need to wait for the completion of the divorce or separation process to gain protection from marital rape.

Ten other states (Alaska, Arizona, Colorado, Idaho, Maine, Montana, New Mexico, Oklahoma, Texas, and Virginia) have a policy that is slightly more protective of wives. In these states the exemption ends once the parties are *living apart*. No bureaucratic action such as obtaining a separation order or filing for a divorce is required in these states. When a wife moves out (or her husband leaves), sexual consent is effectively terminated, and sexual assault by a husband after that point can be construed as rape.

However, in states that limit the exemption in these ways, women still have no protection against a sexual assault at the hands of cohabiting husbands; nor have they any way to withdraw the so-called permanent consent, short of moving out, an alternative that may be blocked if they have no money and nowhere to go. The laws in these states fail to recognize that women can be trapped in marriages, whether by threat or by circumstance. Even when there are no external restrictions on her freedom to leave, it often takes a woman some time to get out of a deteriorating marriage. The situation for wives in such states has been aptly characterized by William O'Donnell of the University of Pittsburgh: "Woe to the wife who is raped before she has her suitcase packed."[3]

The fact that these marital rape exemptions protect some women and fail to protect others has raised the question of whether they may violate the constitution. Up until recently there had been no modern-day constitutional test. In a 1984 decision, however, the New York State Court of Appeals ruled that such exemptions do violate equal protection guarantees.

The New York case, *People v. Liberta* originated when Mario Liberta, a twenty-six year old Buffalo man, was convicted of raping his wife, Denise, from whom he was separated by a court order of protection. New York was one of the states that allowed a rape prosecution if husband and wife were separated under such an order. However, Liberta's attorneys appealed his conviction arguing that *he* was being discriminated against unfairly, since most husbands in New York were exempt from such prosecutions. But instead of agreeing that separated husbands should be treated like other husbands, and given an exemption, the New York high court ruled that there was no justification for special treatment of any husband. The court could find "no rational basis for distinguishing between marital rape and non-marital rape" and declared such distinctions in violation of the equal protection clauses of the federal and state constitutions.

The decision effectively made marital rape a crime under any circumstances and made New York the first state to have its legislated marital rape exemption overturned by a court. This ruling may have far-reaching repercussions. It raised the possibility that challenges may soon be brought and won in other states that have legislated marital-rape exemptions.

Besides the states that have explicitly legislated exemptions (both partial and absolute), there are four jurisdictions that are officially "silent" on the marital-rape matter. Arkansas, Georgia, Mississippi, and the District of Columbia make no mention of a marital-rape exemption in their rape statutes. Until recently, they have been considered common-law jurisdictions with respect to marital rape.[4]

The exact status of the marital-rape exemption in these "silent" states is unclear. Law texts and legal scholars for many years assumed that the common-law tradition supported a marital-rape exemption[5] and that this was the tradition in force in "silent" states.[6] If this were the reigning standard, these "silent" states would, in effect, have a legal situation identical to the most absolute states cited above and would, therefore, bar prosecution of marital rape until divorce has gone through. However, serious questions have been raised, both by legal scholars and now by court decisions, about whether this common-law standard ever really existed and, if it did, whether it applies now.

Dennis Drucker, in a 1979 article for the *Women's Rights Law Reporter*, reviewed the evidence for the existence of a marital-rape exemption in the common-law tradition and found that it rested on a mere handful of cases, all of which he judged either irrelevant or inconclusive.[7] Drucker concluded that the common law did not, after all, support a marital-rape exemption, and argued that when courts began examining the evidence, they would agree with him.

Several influential court opinions have since adopted Drucker's argument. One such opinion was handed down in New Jersey. Prior to 1979, when it removed the spousal exemption, New Jersey was a "silent" state. In 1977, while under the old "silent" statute, a marital-rape case had come before its courts. The case involved a defendant, Albert Smith, who in 1975 broke into the apartment of his estranged wife and allegedly raped and beat her to such an extent that she required hospitalization. When the state prosecuted Smith for rape, a lower court ruled that a rape charge could not be brought because New Jersey's assumed common-law exemption prohibited the prosecution of a husband on a charge of raping his wife.[8]

When the prosecution appealed, the Supreme Court of New Jersey overturned this lower-court opinion, allowing a trial of Smith on the rape charge. In its opinion, the Supreme Court said that it doubted whether an English common-law exemption had ever existed or, if it did, had ever been incorporated into New Jersey law. At the very least, the court said, it did not believe that any common-law exemption went so far as to prohibit the prosecution of a husband, like Smith, who was at the time of the crime separated from his wife. Moreover, the court ruled that no common-law exemption should apply to separated and divorcing women because of changed historical and legal circumstances.

Since the New Jersey decision, courts in two other formerly "silent" states—Massachusetts and Florida—have also held that no common-law marital-rape exemption exists. In Massachusetts, the test case involved James Chretien, who in 1979 broke into his wife's apartment and forced her to have sex with him on the threat that he would kill her if she did not. Chretien and his wife had been separated by judicial decree for a year, and Mrs. Chretien had filed for a divorce that had not yet become final.[9]

Chretien was convicted of rape and sentenced to three to five years in prison, but appealed the conviction to the Supreme Judicial Court of Massachusetts, claiming the common-law spousal exemption. The Supreme Court not only upheld Chretien's conviction, but also substantially clarified the criminal status of marital rape in Massachusetts. The court pointed out that in 1974, when the state legislature revised the rape statutes, it significantly omitted the word "unlawful" in the expression "unlawful intercourse," which is used in the definition of rape. According to the court, by its removal of the word "unlawful" the legislature was recognizing that the only criteria needed to establish rape were the presence of force and the absence of consent. The existence of a marriage did not automatically make intercourse "lawful" and therefore grant husbands immunity from rape prosecution. Moreover, the Massachusetts court also noted that the legislature's earlier enactment of a domestic-violence law that applied to the sexual abuse of a wife indicated the legislature's intention to criminalize marital rape. In Massachusetts, then, not only could an estranged husband like James Chretien be convicted of rape; a cohabiting husband could be convicted, too.

It appears that recent court opinions, along with scholarly research, are challenging the existence of a common-law exemption to prosecution for marital rape. Since marital rape has been ruled a crime in three "silent" states, courts are likely to rule that it is a crime in some of the other "silent" states, too, where the law has yet to be tested. However, as of this writing, the situation in other "silent" states is still undefined.

There are generally considered to be twenty states where cohabiting husbands can clearly be prosecuted for raping their wives. These are California, Connecticut, Delaware, Florida, Hawaii, Iowa, Kansas, Massachusetts, Minnesota, Nebraska, New Hampshire, New Jersey, New York, North Dakota, Oregon, Pennsylvania, Washington, Wisconsin, West Virginia, and Wyoming.

Two of these (Massachusetts and Florida) were formerly silent states where courts have clearly ruled that marital rape is to be considered a crime. In New York, as mentioned earlier, a high court declared the marital rape exemption to be unconstitutional. In the rest, the criminalization has been achieved through legislative action. Not all legislatures have proceeded in the same way. Some, such as Oregon, have simply stricken the exemption across the board. New Jersey has explicitly criminalized marital rape by adding a section to its criminal code regarding sexual offenses: "No actor shall be presumed to be incapable of committing a crime under this chapter because of age or impotency or *marriage to the victim.*"[10] This simple sentence wiped out any claim a husband could make that he was exempt from a sexual offense by virtue of being married to the victim.

Other states have not accomplished the change so cleanly and decisively. Connecticut, for example, passed a law that was intended to criminalize marital rape fully. But several months later, it was discovered that the new law left intact the spousal exemption on several lesser degrees of sexual assault. Similarly, in Iowa, the exemption has been removed from more serious forms of sexual assault but still remains in force in some lesser-sexual-assault statutes.

Instead of trying to eliminate the spousal exemption and make marital rape an offense under ordinary rape statutes, another option is to make marital rape a special crime. California, for example, has taken this route; its criminal code has a special section for marital rape. Under this special law, most husbands cannot claim a marital exemption. However, a husband is still exempted from prosecution for marital rape if his wife does not report the crime to the police within ninety days of the event.[11] He is also exempt if the rape occurred because the victim was incapable of giving consent—in other words, because she was drugged, intoxicated, unconscious, or mentally handicapped. This means that though a man can be convicted of rape if he has sex with an unconscious woman who is not his wife, he is immune if the woman is his wife.

There are two other special provisions of the California marital-rape law. Unlike the ordinary rape law, the marital-rape law in California permits a husband to be charged with a misdemeanor rather than a felony, thus allowing for substantially lesser penalties. Moreover, convicted marital-rapists do not have to register as "sex offenders," as do men convicted of nonmarital rape.

Joanne Schulman and other feminist legal scholars have been critical of the California approach. They argue that by creating a special marital-rape law, a legislature designates marital rape as a less serious crime than nonmarital rape. Schulman favors the New Jersey approach, which simply and expressly eliminates the use of marriage as a defense to charges of rape and makes no other distinction between the kinds of rape. [12]

As we have pointed out, the general trend in recent years appears to have been to limit the marital exemption, either by removing it entirely or by excluding separated and divorcing couples from its purview. But there is an alarming countertrend. Legislators in twelve states have actually taken the initiative to *expand* the marital-rape exemption from its original scope so that it now covers not just husbands but cohabiting boy friends, too. A man in these states who rapes a woman can plead in his defense that he was living with her; even if they had no official marriage license, he can avoid prosecution.

The impulse behind this extension is somewhat understandable, if misguided. More and more couples in the United States are living in nonmarital cohabiting relationships, and many legislators no doubt think that they are modernizing the law by bringing it up to date with social reality. But the irony and injustice of this "modernizing" is that it greatly increases both the number of men who are granted immunity from rape prosecution and the number of women who are left unprotected. As Joanne Schulman suggests, legislators have, apparently, been eager to extend marital protections to men in cohabiting situations while consistently balking at doing the same for women:

> While men in these unmarried cohabiting relationships are increasingly granted the "marital privilege" of rape, women in these relationships have fared far worse in their attempts to obtain privileges of marriage such as spousal support ("palimony"), division of the couple's property or civil orders of protection. In the few states where unmarried women are accorded these rights, courts have first required an express or

implied agreement between the parties. No such requirement is made with respect to the expansion of the marital
rape exemption.[13]

Cohabiting men thus get the legal protections of marriage,
whereas cohabiting women do not. This would appear to be a
clear case of bias based on sex.

A further irony is that cohabiting men have been granted these
privileges as a gift. No large group of cohabiting men has con-
verged on the state houses demanding the right to rape their partners. Whereas, when women's-rights groups have lobbied hard
for laws protecting unmarried cohabiting women, in many instances they have come away empty-handed.

A second kind of insidious expansion of the marital-rape law
has emerged in the form of the "voluntary-social-companion" exemption. These provisions, in force in Delaware, Hawaii, Maine,
North Dakota, and West Virginia, give partial immunity—similar
to the marital exemption—to men who have been permitted previous sexual contact with a woman. Thus, if a man had consensual sex with a woman at some earlier time, he cannot be
convicted of first-degree rape later on.[14] This in effect sanctions
"date rape."

These voluntary-social-companion laws may work to vitiate the
effect of abolishing the marital exemption. For example, when
Delaware eliminated the spousal exemption as it applied to first-
and second-degree rape, it also enacted a law to prohibit the prosecution of voluntary social companions for the crime of first-
degree rape. If "voluntary social companions" are interpreted to
include husbands and cohabiting boy friends, the marital-rape exemption may still be in effect for that first-degree charge.

The expansion of the marital immunity to cover cohabiting and
dating situations is alarming, because it appears to spell even further limitations on a woman's right to determine on her own when
she grants and when she withdraws sexual consent. In the classical Matthew Hale tradition, a man could not be prosecuted for

marital rape because he and his wife had made a formal marriage contract, which in effect implied permanent consent. The extension of the exemption to *cohabitors* appears to imply that a formal contract is no longer necessary to grant the exemption. And the extension of the exemption to voluntary social companions appears to imply that by merely allowing sexual intimacy once, a woman grants a form of permanent consent. These laws spell very large increases in the number of men granted a license to rape.

In summary, then, looking across the United States in recent years, we see contradictory trends. Responding to protests of injustice, some legislatures and courts have responded to the problem of marital rape by restricting or eliminating the marital exemption. Other legislatures and courts, however, have acted to reaffirm the exemption by either defeating reform attempts or by expanding the exemption to cover cohabitors and voluntary social companions.

The sources of these contradictory trends are not difficult to find: they reflect public opinion on the subject. Surveys conducted regarding marital rape in the recent past clearly demonstrate the contradictions around the issue. They show public ambivalence: disapproval of marital rape, but reluctance to use criminal sanctions. They show public division: men pitted against women; the younger generation pitted against the old. And they show public volatility. To predict how the political fortunes of marital rape will fare in state legislatures and courts in the future, it is useful to look at some of these surveys.

If public opinion endorses the notion of a "license to rape" for husbands, it is a subtle kind of license, appearing more as a reluctance to punish than as an outright approval of the use of forced sex. Although it comes as a surprise to some people, polls indicate rather minimal support for the idea that men have an absolute right to sex with their wives. For example, in a 1980 mail survey of 267 Texans, 75 percent of the respondents agreed that a woman had a right to refuse a sexual overture from her hus-band.[15] Twenty-five percent thought otherwise, but at least it can be said that such views are not the norm, at least in Texas.

We ourselves found similar results in our poll of 519 Boston-area residents. We asked, "If a woman refuses more than once in a while to have sex with her husband when he wants it, she is not fulfilling her marital responsibility. Do you agree or disagree?" We posed the question in terms of "marital responsibility" rather than in terms of "rights" because we thought it would tap a more subtle form of the traditional sentiment in favor of the male prerogative. Nonetheless, 69 percent of the sample disagreed, indicating that only a minority in Boston, too, see women as having a "responsi-bility" to perform for their husbands.

Polls also indicate that there is a general repugnance toward the idea of a man's forcing sex on his wife. In the previously cited Texas survey, for example, 90 percent agreed that such acts were "undesirable." We addressed this same issue by asking our re-spondents whether they thought that "if a man uses physical force to have sex with his wife when she doesn't want it, this should be considered rape." Seventy-two percent agreed that the strong term "rape" should apply to such acts. This figure is all the more revealing since the act portrayed as rape was not described as sexual assault: rather, we used the phrase "use of physical force," a description that conjures up less graphic or violent imagery.

The conclusion to be drawn from these two surveys is that there is a generally negative view of men who use force to have sex with their wives. Women are seen as having a right to refuse sex, and when these rights are violated by force, most people are willing to label such acts as rape. But, at the same time, there is other evi-dence suggesting that marital rape is not treated as a serious of-fense in the general hierarchy of offenses. Nor are many people eager to promote public action to prevent and punish it.

One very enlightening piece of evidence that the public mini-mizes the seriousness of marital rape comes from a study of popular attitudes toward crime in general. Peter Rossi, a sociologist, and colleagues presented examples of different crimes to a sample of residents of the city of Baltimore and asked them to rate the crimes' seriousness.[16] The crimes, 140 in all, ranged from hijacking an airplane to refusing to pay a parking fine. Totaling up all the responses, Rossi was able to establish an average score for each on a scale of crime seriousness, and he could also rank each of the 140 crimes based on its score. We have reproduced the rankings here in the table below.

AVERAGE SERIOUSNESS RATINGS
GIVEN TO 140 OFFENSES IN A 1974 BALTIMORE SURVEY

(N is at least 100)
Scores were rated from 9 (most serious) to 1 (least serious)

Rank	Crime	Mean
1	Planned killing of a policeman	8.474
2	Planned killing of a person for a fee	8.406
3	Selling heroin	8.293
4	**Forcible rape after breaking into a home**	**8.241**
5	Impulsive killing of a policeman	8.214
6	Planned killing of a spouse	8.113
7	Planned killing of an acquaintance	8.093
8	Hijacking an airplane	8.072
9	Armed robbery of a bank	8.021
10	Selling LSD	7.949
11	Assault with a gun on a policeman	7.938
12	Kidnapping for ransom	7.930
13	**Forcible rape of a stranger in a park**	**7.909**
14	Killing someone after an argument over a business transaction	7.893
15	Assassination of a public official	7.888
16	Killing someone during a serious argument	7.867

Rank	Crime	Mean
17	Making sexual advances to young children	7.861
18	Assault with a gun on a stranger	7.847
19	Impulsive killing of a spouse	7.835
20	Impulsive killing of a stranger	7.821
21	**Forcible rape of a neighbor**	**7.778**
22	Impulsive killing of an acquaintance	7.717
23	Deliberately starting a fire that results in a death	7.707
24	Assault with a gun on a stranger	7.662
25	Manufacturing and selling drugs known to be harmful to users	7.653
26	Knowingly selling contaminated food that results in a death	7.596
27	Armed robbery of a company payroll	7.577
28	Using heroin	7.520
29	Assault with a gun on an acquaintance	7.505
30	Armed holdup of a taxi driver	7.505
31	**Beating up a child**	**7.490**
32	Armed robbery of a neighborhood druggist	7.487
33	Causing auto accident death while driving when drunk	7.455
34	Selling secret documents to a foreign government	7.423
35	Armed street holdup stealing $200 cash	7.414
36	Killing someone in a bar room free-for-all	7.392
37	Deliberately starting a fire in an occupied building	7.347
38	**Assault with a gun on a spouse**	**7.323**
39	Armed robbery of a supermarket	7.313
40	Assault with a gun in the course of a riot	7.245
41	Armed hijacking of a truck	7.198
42	Deserting to the enemy in time of war	7.194
43	Armed street holdup stealing $25 in cash	7.165
44	Armed robbery of an armored truck	7.163
45	Spying for a foreign government	7.135

Rank	Crime	Mean
46	Killing a pedestrian while exceeding the speed limit	7.122
47	Seduction of a minor	7.021
48	Beating up a policeman	7.020
49	Selling marijuana	6.969
50	**Father-daughter incest**	**6.959**
51	Causing the death of an employee by neglecting to repair machinery	6.918
52	Breaking and entering a bank	6.908
53	Mugging and stealing $25 in cash	6.873
54	Selling pep pills	6.867
55	Cashing stolen payroll checks	6.827
56	Mugging and stealing $200 cash	6.796
57	Causing the death of a tenant by neglecting to repair heating plant	6.704
58	Killing spouse's lover after catching them together	6.691
59	Blackmail	6.667
60	Advocating overthrow of the government	6.663
61	Neglecting to care for own children	6.660
62	**Forcible rape of a former spouse**	**6.653**
63	Manufacturing and selling autos known to be dangerously defective	6.604
64	**Beating up a stranger**	**6.604**
65	Using LSD	6.557
66	Driving while drunk	6.545
67	Practicing medicine without a license	6.500
68	Burglary of a home stealing a color TV set	6.440
69	Knowingly passing counterfeit money	6.392
70	Beating up someone in a riot	6.368
71	Performing illegal abortions	6.330
72	Passing worthless checks for more than $500	6.309
73	A public official accepting bribes in return for favors	6.240
74	Employee embezzling company funds	6.207

Rank	Crime	Mean
75	Knowingly selling stolen stocks and bonds	6.138
76	Refusing to obey lawful order of a policeman	6.118
77	Burglary of a home stealing a portable transistor radio	6.115
78	Theft of a car for the purpose of resale	6.093
79	Knowingly selling defective used cars as completely safe	6.093
80	Burglary of an appliance store stealing several TV sets	6.062
81	Looting goods in a riot	6.043
82	Knowingly selling stolen goods	6.021
83	Leaving the scene of an accident	5.949
84	Printing counterfeit $10 bills	5.948
85	Shoplifting a diamond ring from a jewelry store	5.939
86	**Mother-son incest**	**5.907**
87	Theft of a car for joy-riding	5.876
88	Intimidating a witness in a court case	5.853
89	**Brother-sister incest**	**5.825**
90	Knowingly selling worthless stocks as valuable investments	5.821
91	**Beating up a spouse**	**5.796**
92	Selling liquor to minors	5.789
93	Burglary of a factory stealing machine tools	5.789
94	Using stolen credit cards	5.750
95	Using pep pills	5.656
96	Joining a riot	5.656
97	Lending money at illegal interest rates	5.653
98	Knowingly buying stolen goods	5.596
99	Refusal to serve when drafted in peace time	5.535
100	Resisting arrest	5.449
101	Impersonating a policeman	5.449
102	Using false identification to obtain goods from a store	5.438
103	Bribing a public official to obtain favors	5.394
104	Passing worthless checks involving less than $100	5.339

Rank	Crime	Mean
105	Desertion from military service in peace time	5.323
106	Under-reporting income on income tax returns	5.305
107	Willfully neglecting to file income tax returns	5.157
108	Soliciting for prostitution	5.144
109	Proposing homosexual practices to an adult	5.140
110	Overcharging on repairs to automobiles	5.135
111	Shoplifting a dress from a department store	5.070
112	**Beating up an acquaintance**	**5.032**
113	Driving while license is suspended	5.031
114	Pouring paint over someone's car	4.938
115	Shoplifting a pair of shoes from a shoe store	4.990
116	Overcharging for credit in selling goods	4.970
117	Shoplifting a carton of cigarettes from a supermarket	4.969
118	Smuggling goods to avoid paying import duties	4.918
119	Killing a suspected burglar in home	4.868
120	False claims of dependents on income tax return	4.832
121	Knowingly using inaccurate scales in weighing meat for sale	4.786
122	Refusal to make essential repairs to rental property	4.781
123	Engaging in male homosexual acts with consenting adults	4.736
124	Engaging in female homosexual acts with consenting adults	4.729
125	Breaking a plate glass window in a shop	4.653
126	Fixing prices of a consumer product like gasoline	4.629
127	Fixing prices of machines sold to businesses	4.619
128	Selling pornographic magazines	4.526
129	Shoplifting a book in a bookstore	4.424
130	Repeated refusal to obey parents	4.411
131	Joining a prohibited demonstration	4.323
132	False advertising of headache remedy	4.083
133	Refusal to pay alimony	4.063

Rank	Crime	Mean
134	Refusal to pay parking fines	3.583
135	Disturbing the peace	3.779
136	Repeated truancy	3.573
137	Repeated running away from home	3.571
138	Loitering in public places	3.375
139	Refusal to answer census taker	3.105
140	Being drunk in public places	2.849

The most serious kinds of crimes, not surprisingly, were murders, especially planned killings. Five of the ten most serious crimes were murders of some sort. Rape was also considered a very serious offense on this scale. "Forcible rape after breaking into a home" was considered the fourth-most-serious offense, rated just higher than the impulsive killing of a policeman. All the rape vignettes except one were listed in the top twenty-five crimes, and they were quite closely matched in seriousness with crimes involving killing. The residents of Baltimore obviously considered rape among the most serious of crimes.

Conspicuous for its low ranking in this list of 140 cases, however, was the crime "forcible rape of a former spouse." It ranked sixty-second in the list, two below "advocating overthrow of the government" and a few above "driving while drunk." "Forcible rape of a former spouse" was not treated as an insignificant crime—it could have been rated much lower, down with using pep pills (number 95), shoplifting (111), or refusing to pay parking fines (134). But it is evident that it is not at all in the same range as other crimes of sexual assault, all of which were located in the top twenty-five.

What we do not know is where the citizens of Baltimore would have ranked the crime "forcible rape of a current spouse." For some reason, possibly because it was not an illegal offense in Maryland at the time, Rossi and his colleagues did not ask about it. However, if "forcible rape of a former spouse" was ranked forty places below any other rape, we suspect "forcible rape of a current spouse" would be ranked still lower, since the fact that the victim of a rape was at one time a spouse—that alone, with no other information about the crime—was cause to demote the seriousness of the act substantially in the minds of most ordinary citizens.

In another study, two sociologists in San Antonio, Texas, Joyce Williams and Karen Holmes, interviewed nearly a thousand of that city's residents about different kinds of rape.[17] They showed each interviewee a card with a description of a rape incident printed on it, and asked questions about it. The incidents included rape by a stranger, rape by an acquaintance, rape of a prostitute, and rape of a wife by her husband. The husband-wife scenario read as follows: "A husband and wife had an argument. The husband was very angry so he went to a bar to have a few drinks. After several hours he returned home to find his wife asleep. He woke her up and demanded that she have sex with him. She refused, but he slapped her across the face and, although she resisted, forced her to have sexual relations with him." As with Rossi's study, respondents rated this incident the least serious of all the sexual assaults, by a large margin. Only half the sample, in fact, were willing to define it as rape at all. And when subjects were asked whether the husband should be prosecuted, the percentages got even smaller. Only 29 percent of the men and 42 percent of the women thought prosecution should take place. Even a third of the men and women who thought the act was a rape were unwilling to see any action taken. In many people's minds, marital rape is a crime that no one should do anything about.

The reluctance to take official action against marital rape also shows up in some polls regarding legal changes. In one mail survey, also done in Texas, two thousand respondents were asked, "Are you in favor of Texas having a law that permits a wife to accuse her husband of rape?"[18] Only 35 percent said yes, which suggests widespread antipathy toward criminalizing marital rape.

However, there is other evidence that opinions about criminalizing marital rape may differ from place to place and from survey to survey. The University of Hartford did a telephone survey in the summer of 1981 of 475 people in the greater Hartford area on a variety of subjects including marital rape.[19] In this survey, respondents were asked whether they favored the new Connecticut law (passed only the previous spring) that allowed a woman to charge her husband or cohabiting lover with rape. In this survey, 67 percent, or exactly two-thirds, said they were in favor of the law.

The dramatic difference between the Connecticut poll and the Texas poll on the subject of criminalizing marital rape highlights the difficulty in gauging public opinion precisely on this subject. It is hard to get an exact reading of where public opinion stands, for a number of reasons. First, the mention of marital rape raises a conflicting variety of images and elicits different kinds of responses, depending on how the question is asked. The Texas poll, for example, asked, "Are you in favor of a law that permits a wife to accuse her husband of rape?" The question is, unfortunately, posed in a way that heavily biases the response. The whole sentence, for example, speaks only of an accusation, not an event; the respondent understandably wonders whether anything actually happened. No one wants to encourage "accusations," which have a generally negative connotation; the image of a vindictive wife bringing accusations against an innocent husband comes too easily to mind. This may be one reason that the Texas poll showed so little support for a marital-rape law.

Another difficulty with pinning down opinions about marital rape is that most people have scarcely thought about the problem. Thus, people's opinions are likely to be very volatile. If they read an article on the subject in the paper two days after they are polled, their opinion may do a 180-degree reversal.

The Texas poll, for example, was taken in 1979, just after the Rideout case but prior to many of the media discussions about the issue. (For more on the Rideout case, see Chapter 9.) The Connecticut poll was completed almost two years later, after a spring in which the Connecticut public had been exposed to a host of newspaper articles about marital rape and the prospect of their state legislature's passing a new law on the subject. It is understandable that Hartford residents had different attitudes toward marital rape from the Texans.

Another possible explanation of the divergence between the two surveys rests in state and regional differences. Texas is a politically conservative state and had at the time one of the most archaic statutes in the country on the subject of marital rape.

Connecticut, by contrast, is a traditionally liberal state. It was the first state in the country to elect a woman governor in her own right (not as a replacement for her husband). Two other New England states, New Hampshire and Massachusetts, have now eliminated the marital-rape exemption. It is likely that attitudes in Connecticut, and New England in general, are more favorable to public intervention than in Texas.

There are other differences besides regional ones in the support for the criminalization of marital rape. Opinion on marital rape divides the sexes, and this split shows up in all kinds of inquiries on this subject. In the Connecticut poll, 77 percent of the women approved of the new state law, compared with only 55 percent of the men.[20] In Texas, 45 percent of the women wanted the state to allow prosecution of husbands, compared with only 25 percent of the men.[21] In San Antonio, of those shown the vignette where the husband assaults the wife, 61 percent of the women called it rape, but only 43 percent of the men.[22] Women obviously identify with the victims and want protection.

The difference of opinion also runs along generational lines. More young people than older people see something wrong with forced sex in marriage and want legal action to criminalize it. In the Texas opinion poll, for example, the gap was quite big: 59 percent of the women under forty supported a new state law, but only 33 percent of the women over forty agreed with them.[23] Younger women (and also younger men) are more favorable to the feminist position. This is another reason to think change in the law will be enjoying increasing popular support as time goes on.

Support for criminalization of marital rape is also correlated with liberal attitudes toward sex roles, low levels of religious participation, and patterns of female employment. People who are highly religious seem to be skeptical of changing the law regarding the marital-rape exemption.[25] This may have to do with the traditional attitudes about male domination that have been supported by certain organized religious groups in the past. By contrast, women who work and men whose wives work all express more support for criminalizing marital rape, as do persons who show liberal attitudes toward the role of women in society and the family.[25] What this seems to show is that there is some interconnection among profeminist ideas—from the ERA, to working wives, to prosecution for marital rape.

Profeminist attitudes, especially on the matter of rape, tend to be somewhat more common among the better educated.[26] So it is not surprising that men and women with higher educations were more likely to consider a forced-sex episode as marital rape in our Boston study. They were also less likely to endorse the idea that a wife has any sexual obligation to perform for her husband.

Perhaps the only unexpected difference of opinion on the marital-rape issue comes on the matter of race. Nonwhites seem to be more opposed to criminalizing marital rape than whites.[27] The careful analysis by Texas sociologists Williams and Holmes suggests, however, that the difference by race is almost entirely due to the attitudes of the men. Nonwhite females do not differ much on this issue from their white sisters, but minority men seem so adamantly opposed to criminalization of marital rape that they pull down the whole score for nonwhites on this subject.

Of course, the strong negative reaction of minority men to the criminalization of marital rape may have to do with the historic discrimination that black men have suffered at the hands of the rape law. Rape charges were traditionally used, especially in the

South, to persecute blacks and to spur lynchings. And there is evidence that today, in all parts of the country, racial bias still operates to impose heavier legal sanctions on black rapists (and other black offenders) than on whites.[28] It is not surprising that the group most opposed to the creation of such a new law is the group most legitimately concerned about being the prime target of its use.

Because it is a topical subject, polls on marital rape will continue to appear, and we expect they will show a variety of responses, for some of the reasons discussed earlier—the wording of questions, prior media treatment of the subject, and regional variation. Over the long run, however, as the issue gains in visibility and familiarity, we believe that the polls will show increasing public support for the elimination of the spousal exemption. State laws will reflect this growing public opinion and, in time, although the process may be slow, we believe the criminalization of marital rape will become the rule rather than the exception.

9

The Debate Over Criminalizing Marital Rape

Marriage was for life and women were considered to be the property of their husbands when, in the seventeenth century, British jurist Matthew Hale made his famous pronouncement exempting husbands from prosecution for marital rape.[1] It has stood for three centuries as the most often quoted reason why husbands should be immune from prosecution for rape.

It is now generally acknowledged that Hale, for all his legal erudition, was a rabid woman-hater who made his mark among his contemporaries by burning women at the stake as witches.[2] It also goes without saying that the conception of matrimony and the rights of women have changed a great deal since Hale's day. Yet his famous dictum has been cited as the legal gospel on marital rape from his time until the present, virtually without challenge.

Hale's dictum appeals in its logic to two common-sense notions, and therein, perhaps, lies its popularity. One is the idea that marriage implies a special agreement for sexual intimacy. Hale articulated this as a "consent" by which a wife "hath given herself . . . unto her husband, which she cannot retract." The second is the idea that for rape to occur there must be an absence of consent. If a form of consent exists between a husband and a wife when intercourse occurs, a rape cannot be said to have taken place.

Of course, there turns out to be a great deal more to the issue than this simple logic at first suggests. Only recently have commentators begun to scrutinize Hale's logic more seriously, and they suggest that it masks questions about consent, harm, inequality, and illegitimate force. Under rigorous consideration Hale's notions hardly stand up to our contemporary standards of justice and ethics, and probably ought to be discarded. Because Hale's ideas have so dominated the legal discussion of marital rape, we want to review here some of the criticisms that have been leveled at his notion of "permanent consent," as it has come to be called.

Hale argued that marriage implies a consent to sex. Most of the modern critics of Hale's idea have pointed out emphatically that though a woman, by marrying, may be consenting to sex, she is most certainly not consenting to rape.[3] In other words, she cannot be giving him permission to harm her, to force her, or to humiliate her. Hale's argument, as Professor Martin Schwartz lampoons it, "assumes that the wife has given consent to sexual intercourse at Yankee stadium between games of a double-header."[4]

Hale may, indeed, have meant consent to apply to such extreme situations. In one nineteenth-century British case that applied Hale's theory, a woman brought her husband to court because he had knowingly infected her with gonorrhea. She argued that had she realized he was diseased, she would have never consented to have sex with him. Eleven English judges hearing the case disagreed. They ruled that the husband was not guilty of harming her because it was not illegal for him to force his wife to have intercourse even if he was knowingly hurting her. One of the justices, in fact, argued that a "wife never has the right nor the power to refuse, no matter how much she should suffer, even when her husband's conduct amounts to cruelty."[5] In his view, a married woman did consent to be harmed.

This kind of interpretation has seemed too barbaric for most modern legal thinkers. Even if they grant that marriage implies consent to sex, they will acknowledge that the imposition of harm nullifies any such consent. A 1967 opinion by an Israeli judge expresses this position:

> In my view, this doctrine does not do justice to the dignity of man nor the dignity of matrimony. . . . Even though a woman agrees by her marriage to live with her husband as man and wife, she does not thereby agree to suffer severe bodily harm. A wife is not like a "captive taken with the sword" in her husband's house and she has the same right of corporal freedom as he. If she should, without sufficient reason, refuse to maintain matrimonial relations with her husband, he has such legal remedies as the personal law of the parties provides; but no one is allowed to take the law into his own hands and enforce his right by an act of violence.[6]

Whatever may have been the situation in Victorian England, it is unlikely that there would be widespread support in modern-day America for the idea that, in marrying, a woman consents to being willfully infected with gonorrhea or otherwise done bodily harm. To reinforce this point, legal scholar Marianne Stecich has pointed out that our modern law in general does not allow people to consent to harm.[7] In cases where students were injured in the course of fraternity hazings, for example, courts have thrown out the argument that the students "consented" to harm when they agreed to undergo the hazing. She cites an even more pertinent example, where a husband justified his actions in a wife-beating case by contending to the court that his wife had "consented" to the beating. The court disagreed. It ruled, in effect, that even if she had said, "Go ahead and beat me," this did not give him the right to do so. Whatever consent to sex is implied in the marriage vows, consent to harm is not part of it.

The Israeli judge makes another telling point in his eloquent quote, cited earlier. "No one is allowed to take the law into his own hands and enforce his right by an act of violence," he says. In other words, even if marriage does grant permanent consent and the woman has no grounds for denying her husband's request for sex, this does not give him grounds to use force to compel her. She may be wrong, but if he rapes her, he is also wrong.

Joanne Schulman, of the National Center on Women and Family Law, illustrates this point with the following analogy. Suppose you have a contract for the delivery of some tools by a certain date, but your supplier fails to make his delivery on time. Of course he is in violation of his contract. But that does not give you the privilege of breaking into his warehouse and taking the tools by force. You have to go to court to enforce your contract.[8]

Other critics of Hale's notion of permanent consent have questioned how permanent, in fact, this consent really is. Hale's dictum itself has the icy ring of a prison sentence in its phrase "consent . . . which she cannot retract." Most modern legal commentators agree that a serious defect in the permanent-consent notion is contained in this idea that consent is unretractable.

"How can one logically defend the result—that a husband has an unbridled right, *protected by law*, to force himself sexually upon her at any time he chooses, no matter how far the marriage relationship has deteriorated between them."[9] Although Judge Scalera, in making this pronouncement, did not quite see fit to order the defendant in the marital-rape case of New Jersey v. Albert Smith (1979) to stand trial, he did articulate one of the most common objections to the permanent consent idea.

In Hale's day, marriage itself could not be retracted. In our day, we have not only liberalized the institution of divorce to spare many husbands and wives years of suffering, but we also recognize that the mutuality may depart from a marriage even before a couple divorces. There is widespread agreement that couples should be allowed to terminate the institution of marriage and the rights and privileges attendant to it, including consent to sex.

Many states have taken this critique of the permanent-consent doctrine to heart and imposed restrictions on the marital-rape exemption, the most common of which is to specify that it ceases to apply at some point during the break-up of a couple's relationship, either when they begin to live separately or when they file for a divorce (see Chapter 8). So instead of a permanent consent we have in many states what might be termed a doctrine of quasi-permanent consent, a consent that may be retracted.

Still other criticism has been directed at the Hale doctrine and its idea of what is meant by consent. Consent is usually defined as "permission" or "agreement," but in the Hale tradition consent has been taken to mean not just that the wife agrees to have sex, but that she has a duty to do so on demand.

Public-opinion surveys indicate that a certain minority of the population thinks this is what marriage means. And some element of the legal community makes this interpretation, too: "Forced intercourse is one of the woman's matrimonial duties under the law and this assumption is virtually universal in the Western world."[10] But other legal scholars disagree. They see no duty to provide sex on demand implied in our laws.

Marianne Stecich, writing one of the first feminist commentaries on the marital-rape exemption, points out that, apart from the marital-rape law inspired by Hale, there are virtually no cases from the area of family law that would imply that, in marriage, whenever they desire, men have a right to sex and women have a duty to perform.[11] In fact she cites many cases where the law would appear to imply the contrary. For example, divorces have been granted to women on the grounds of "excessive sexual demands by the husband." This suggests that a woman has a right to refuse if she thinks a husband wants sex too often.

If we look at it from another angle, we see that other courts have failed to grant divorces to men who sought them solely on the grounds that their wives refused to have sex for a certain period of time. Here again the decisions imply that a simple refusal by a woman to have sex on some occasions does not violate the contract implied in marriage. So the notion of a marital duty to perform sex may not really have as much foundation in American law as it seems to in male folk culture.

Unfortunately, the law is not totally consistent on the questions of what sexual rights and duties are implied in marriage, and understandably so. Even if people did not mind airing such personal matters in public, sexual grievances are not the kind that they see much point in litigating in a courtroom. Divorce or sex counseling seems a more pertinent solution. In consequence, courts have fairly few opportunities to give opinions on these private issues. Moreover, it is understandable why legislatures have not spelled out the issue in greater detail, either. Any legislature that would try to take on such a task would create such furor that few of its members would likely survive another election. It is not surprising that judges and politicians have left this Pandora's box closed.

However, agitation from the women's movement is challenging legislatures across the country to repudiate Hale's doctrine and eliminate the spousal exemption. In New Jersey, for example, a reform passed rather readily, though in other states, such as New York and Michigan, stiff opposition to criminalizing marital rape was encountered.

But the vociferous opponents of the new marital-rape laws have, in general, not defended the status quo with the logic of Matthew Hale. They have not eagerly insisted that matrimony grants a man the permanent consent to sex. Instead, the most popular arguments against marital-rape bills in recent years have been about the operation of the *legal* system. Opponents do not insist any longer that rape is impossible in marriage, or that permanent consent gives a husband the right to use force. Rather, they argue that new laws are not necessary, or that they will not work, or that they will ruin family life. It is not that the concept of marital rape is wrong, these opponents say, just that a new law is not the way to remedy the problem.

These new arguments signify a kind of retreat. Whereas its supporters once felt comfortable defending the spousal-rape exemption on philosophical grounds, they have lately been forced to fight for their cause on matters of administrative expediency. They no longer argue openly in behalf of their conception of marriage but, instead, raise alarms about the operation of the legal system. It is a sign that some of the moral conviction has departed from their defense. Still, the new arguments are taken seriously by many people and have been given impassioned voice by certain legislators and attorneys. They deserve serious discussion.

Probably the most passionately held "new argument" against defining marital rape as a crime is that it will lead to frivolous complaints by vindictive women. Alfred Onorato, a member of the Connecticut General Court, is convinced of this peril:

> The jails are full of guys because of vengeful wives, and there are a lot of them. . . . A lot of these cases are pumped through the court system because the wives are angry at the husbands. The guy stayed out too late or he was running around with other women. And since society is already burdened with these kinds of women, the *last* thing we need is a law making it illegal for a husband to sexually assault his wife. . . . Giving a wife the opportunity to charge her husband with sexual assault? That would *really* open the floodgates.[12]

Although clearly questionable, this argument needs to be taken seriously because it is aimed at a very powerful audience: police and prosecutors. The opinions of police and prosecutors have great weight with legislators on matters of criminal law. After all, it is they who have to enforce these laws. If police and prosecutors vociferously oppose making marital rape a crime because they believe the legal system will be swamped, legislators will be that much more reluctant to act.

Law-enforcement officers are already hesitant to get involved in family crimes. In the view of many of them, such crimes are complicated, time-consuming, and full of pitfalls.[13] Many police officers readily recall the wife in their precinct who would summon the squad car to her home every Saturday night but would complain bitterly when they carted her husband off to jail. Many prosecutors say they have a vivid memory of a solid case they built against a chronic wife-beater, only, at the last moment, to have the tearful wife drop the charges. Her husband is really a good man. She has forgiven him and they want to get back together. Police and prosecutors often see domestic crimes as a nuisance and a waste of their time. So, when opponents of marital-rape law reform talk about a rash of frivolous and vindictive complaints, it can strike a responsive chord.

However plausible they may sound, these concerns about frivolous charges have little supporting evidence. Their plausibility arises less from any real experience than from the reservoir of negative stereotypes that many men hold about rape victims.[14] In fact, experience with current marital-rape laws and marital-rape prosecutions suggests that they are not used frivolously. If anything, they are underused. A glance around the country and abroad bears this out.

Sweden, for example, has had a law making marital rape a crime for over fifteen years. Criminologist Gilbert Geis went to Sweden in 1979 to find out how the law was working. No one at any level of society in Sweden thought the marital-rape laws were being abused. After searching the records, he was able to come up with only four examples of such prosecutions for the year 1970 and two for the year 1976. There was no evidence of a large number of frivolous complaints.[15]

Closer to home, a look at the American states that have dropped the marital-rape exemption reveals the same results. Nebraska, for example, which eliminated the exemption in 1976, had not had a single prosecution under it six years later. Oregon, up to 1982, had only had four. In California, the most populous state in the country, we could locate only forty-two cases for the years 1980–81, and even a cursory look at this relatively large sample (see Appendix B) shows them to be almost entirely made up of well-documented and brutal crimes, not quarrels between spouses that happened to spill into the courts.

Those who incite the fear of frivolous rape charges often point to the infamous Rideout case in Oregon, where, in 1978, a complaint of rape led to a long and bitter trial. The case concerned a couple in their early twenties, John and Greta Rideout.[16] Their four-year relationship had generally been stormy, punctuated by a number of separations and reconciliations and marred by episodes of violence by John against Greta.

The trial itself revolved around an incident that occurred on October 10, 1978. According to testimony given by Greta, John awoke from a nap that afternoon and demanded that Greta have sex with him. Having become increasingly alienated from John in recent days because of his violence, his depressive withdrawals, his extramarital affairs, and his threats to throw her and her daughter out, she said no. John, however, refused to accept her refusal, and when he became aggressive, Greta ran out of the house. She tried to hide and run away, but John caught her and dragged her back to the house. Then, under a rain of threats and blows, he tore her pants off, forced her to the floor, and had sex with her.

After the forced sex, Greta managed to escape and went to a neighbor's home and then to the police, who told her she needed to wait two days under Oregon law to file a rape charge. Greta got in touch with a counselor at the Salem Women's Crisis Center, who helped her get to the hospital so that the doctors could document Greta's bruises and the fact that her vagina showed signs of sexual assault. Two days later, Greta filed charges against her husband; a week after that, John was arrested and charged with rape (Oregon was one of only three states where a cohabiting husband could be prosecuted in 1978). Two months later, a jury was selected to hear the case and the trial began.

The Rideout case was *not* the first instance in the United States of a man being prosecuted for raping his wife. A New Jersey man, Daniel Morrison, had been found guilty of raping his wife and sentenced to four to twelve years in jail on May 15, 1978, six months before the Rideout case. But Rideout was the first husband still effectively living with his wife to be tried for marital rape. The case was widely publicized as the first marital-rape trial, and it received an enormous amount of national media attention. Newspapers ran stories on the trial and its aftermath for nearly a full month; editorials were written, pro and con; the Rideouts were featured on a national network talk show; a special two-hour TV movie was made about the events and the subsequent trial. The Rideout case became a true national spectacle.

The defense, trying to paint Greta as a disturbed and vindictive woman, brought evidence that she had once before told John about a sexual assault (by her brother-in-law) which she had later retracted (Greta said she had been intimidated by the brother-in-law into retracting); and also that she had told John about a lesbian fantasy, which she later denied (Greta said she was not a lesbian but was trying to lure John into talking about his own homosexual interests). In the face of such discrediting testimony, the jury chose to overlook medical evidence that the assault had occurred and decided that there was too much doubt to convict John of the charges. He was freed. Then, several days later, to the surprise of many, the couple met, effected a reconciliation, and decided to move back together.

The outcome of the trial and the subsequent events angered and disappointed many who had hoped that the trial would be an important victory for the cause of marital-rape reform. Instead, the Rideouts' reconciliation played into arguments of skeptics who claimed it proved that vindictive wives would only use rape laws to harass husbands and waste prosecutors' time with cases that were better handled in a divorce court or marriage counseling. However, knowledgeable observers believe the problem in the Rideout trial was not with either a vindictive wife or a defective law but, rather, with the trial attorneys. Shortly after the case came to public attention, for example, John's defense team was joined by Charles Burt, a prominent Oregon attorney who had a strong conviction that husbands should be exempt from prosecution for rape. Believing that the Oregon law was bad, he was intent on defeating it in the courts. Burt took his case straight to the media, and his pronouncements were soon being quoted by reporters and attacked by feminists, all of which fueled the notoriety of both sides of this *cause célèbre*.

There was also much hostility focused on the prosecutor, Gary Gortmaker, who was seen as having compromised the case because of his lukewarm commitment to the principle in the first place. (He was quoted as saying before the trial, "If it had happened in the bedroom and he didn't beat her up, I'd agree with the other side."[17]) He was also criticized for having made strategic errors in the prosecution, thus ensuring John's acquittal.

Peter Sandrock, a district attorney from a neighboring Oregon county, later wrote to a Connecticut legislator, "The merits of the [Rideout] case aside, the prosecutor in that case . . . has since been convicted of multiple felonies involving abuse of his office. Having prosecuted a spousal rape in [my own] county, I can assure you that Rideout was an unnecessary debacle created by the trial attorneys."[18]

Moreover, in spite of John Rideout's acquittal, there was other evidence that he was a violent and abusive man. He admitted to hitting Greta on occasion and even hinted after the trial that he had actually committed the rape. Later, after a second separation, he was arrested for breaking into her house and assaulting her.

This time he was convicted of criminal trespass and placed on probation; when he violated the terms of his probation by harassing Greta, he eventually spent three months in jail. Prosecuting such a man would hardly qualify as "frivolous." Moreover, the fact that there are acquittals under any law does not mean that the law is being misused. It means only that American jurisprudence, in its zeal to protect the rights of the accused, requires proof "beyond a reasonable doubt" to gain conviction for criminal offenses. It can be taken as a healthy sign, not as proof that marital-rape prosecutions are a waste.

Though critics often point to the Rideout case, they usually fail to note that there has been no hue and cry from beleaguered prosecutors charged with carrying out these new marital-rape laws. In fact, the laws have earned more praise than condemnation from those in a position to use them. The district attorney quoted above is so convinced that the law works well that he has testified in behalf of marital-rape laws in other states. He writes about the experience in Oregon: "The one thing that has *not* happened . . . is that embittered and vengeful wives are rushing to their District Attorneys to falsely claim rape in order to gain leverage on their husbands in a divorce."[19] "Oregon has experienced neither a significant rise in spousal rape complaints, nor the use of the rape charge by vindictive wives to extort financial or other concessions."[20]

The small number of marital-rape complaints in states such as Oregon comes as little surprise to those familiar with rape victims. Rape is one of the most—if not *the* most—underreported crimes in America since rape prosecutions usually cause as much hardship to the victim as they do to the offender.[21] Rape victims suffer from the public exposure of their personal lives and from the abrasive skepticism of police and defense attorneys. All this makes reporting a rape complaint a troubling decision for the victim of a stranger-rape. It is little wonder that women who have been raped by their husbands rarely consider the idea of pressing charges. As one observer noted, "The self-exposure required and insensitive treatment by police and media that could be expected are deterrents to any report of marital rape, let alone false ones."[22]

Also, if vindictive wives are inclined to bring frivolous charges, as some have argued, then why aren't they doing it already—with other crimes? After all, wives can currently have their husbands prosecuted for an array of crimes such as theft, kidnapping, incest, sodomy, forgery, and so forth. "Clearly a woman set on revenge could choose a method less embarrassing to herself (and more likely of success) than a marital rape prosecution," points out attorney Moira Griffin.[23] But such frivolous charges are unusual. They are infrequently brought on these other criminal grounds, and they would be just as unlikely to be brought on the grounds of marital rape.

Undoubtedly, some false complaints of marital rape will be brought, just as with any crime; false charges are always a possibility under the criminal law. However, "if potential false charges were reason not to legislate against certain actions, there wouldn't be a law on the books," says Griffin. Fortunately, the legal system includes elaborate precautions and protections to deal with false charges. At the lowest level there is the police investigation to determine if a crime occurred. Then prosecutors have considerable discretion about whether or not to prosecute, depending on whether they believe a case is serious. There is also the jury's power to determine the credibility of the witnesses and obligation to base a conviction on a standard of "proof beyond a reasonable doubt." We are apparently content to allow these procedures to weed out false claims in all other areas of the criminal law. Why should it be any different with marital rape?

Part of the problem rests in the persistent cultural stereotype that women are vindictive.[24] This notion that women are prone to making false charges is evident in those rape statutes that require that another witness corroborate the victim's testimony—a corroboration not required for any other type of assault. The attitude is reflected succinctly in the comments of Charles Burt: "If these [marital-rape] laws are enacted across the country, we're going to have an incredible legal mess. . . . With this law a woman can say 'give me what I want, my dear, or it's going to cost you ten grand to defend yourself when I scream rape.' "[25]

Matthew Hale himself institutionalized this suspicious view of women with his warning "Rape is an accusation easily to be made and hard to be proved, and harder to be defended by the party accused, tho' never so innocent," which many states have required judges to read to juries in all rape trials.

But all available evidence points in the other direction: rape is an accusation difficult to *make*. Research suggests that from four out of five to nine out of ten rapes go unreported.[26] Rape prosecutions have among the lowest conviction rates of all serious crimes.[27] Rapes involving acquaintances and intimates are the least likely to be reported and the least likely to result in a conviction. The argument that it would be easy for wives to press charges against husbands when they had no legitimate complaint is unsubstantiated, relying on stereotype rather than fact for the credibility that it still carries.

A second argument many people currently use to oppose marital-rape law reform is that the crime will be impossible to prove (or refute). Imagine how much more difficult it will be to prove when the parties are husband and wife, when they have had consensual sex hundreds of times before, when there are thousands of possible motives for false charges, and when nobody will have witnessed the rape. It will never be anything more than her word against his, and what jury will convict on the basis of that?

Once again, the evidence from the states where marital rape is a crime contradicts this logic. Success rates in prosecutions for marital rape have been running high. In Oregon, three out of the four prosecutions brought before July 1982 resulted in conviction.[28] In California, of twenty-eight cases that went to court between January 1980 and December 1981, there were twenty-five convictions (see Appendix B). Even when offenders were not convicted of marital rape, often the marital-rape charge was used effectively by the prosecutor to bargain for a guilty plea on a lesser charge of felonious assault or kidnapping.

So marital rape is not impossible to prove. The kinds of cases being brought under the marital-rape laws are often the most brutal and flagrant ones. They include cases like that of Andrew Jackson Armstead, who was convicted by a jury in November 1981 of raping his wife. Armstead had placed a gun in his wife's mouth and threatened to pull the trigger if she did not have sex with him.[29] He was found in the morning by the police, still in his wife's bed, with a gun nearby. Marital-rapists do get caught with evidence of their crimes. Often their wives have graphic injuries, or there is evidence of hideous sexual abuse, or witnesses overhear the offenses and can corroborate the stories. Contrary to dire predictions, prosecutions against husband-rapists have been resulting in convictions.

Obviously, some of these cases are unusual, both in their level of brutality and in the circumstances that permitted the corroboration of the woman's story. They hardly prove that marital rape is an easy charge to substantiate, but they do show that there are plenty of uses for the law. Even if it only ends up applying to a handful of cases every year, these cases warrant a law against marital rape.

But the difficulty-of-proof argument is suspect on other grounds, too. Suppose there were *no* easy-to-prove cases of marital rape and most cases *did* boil down to a matter of her word against his. This is not sufficient reason for not criminalizing marital rape. It might be a good reason for prosecutors and police to do a more thorough investigation or for judges to issue cautions to juries. But difficulty of proof has never been a proper criterion for deciding what behavior should be officially censured by society.

Our law censures many kinds of crimes that are difficult to prove. Incest, for example, represents an analogous situation, in that many complaints are based on little more than the word of a daughter pitted against the word of the father. Proving the charge in incest cases is even more difficult than in marital rape because the daughter, as a child, will have little credibility in the eyes of jurors, and many of the other family members—such as mothers and siblings—are only too eager to discredit her in order to "save their family."[30]

Without a doubt, some marital-rape cases will be difficult to prove. The wife-complainant will certainly suffer under the burden of much prejudice. Juries are likely to be skeptical, much more skeptical than in the case of a stranger-rape. Obviously, police, prosecutors, and complainants will have to work extra hard to make their cases convincing. But if an act is morally and legally abhorrent, it should be a crime.

Opponents of marital-rape law reform often claim that it will have a negative impact on the family, that it will further pave the increasingly easy and tempting road to divorce. "It would not help the marital situation to send the husband off to prison," said Ralph Slovenko, professor of law at Wayne State University.[31] "By weakening the resolve of the partners to repair the crack in their marriage, criminal charges would act like a sledge hammer on a wedge," said David Phillips, an Australian commentator.[32]

In fact, there is truth to this claim: a couple may indeed be less likely to "kiss and make up" if the wife has just brought rape charges against her husband. But this is not necessarily bad. Those who worry that marital-rape prosecutions may destroy marriage have a distorted view of these disintegrating marriages. We are asked to imagine an essentially loving and healthy relationship that has been marred by one minor mistake, a mistake that then gets stretched all out of proportion by the heavy hand of the law.

Unfortunately, this is not an accurate description of the kind of marriages out of which marital-rape prosecutions emerge. As we have shown, many of the wives have been victims of violence for years. Many are trapped in their marriages by fear and economic circumstances. The woman who finally gets up the nerve to go to the police with a complaint of rape against her husband has not simply experienced an unusual marital squabble. In most cases, she is a woman who has been abused before.

Naturally, if the state deprives this woman of the possibility of prosecuting her husband for rape, her marriage may be more likely to endure. Without the social support of a criminal law stating that she has been wronged, she may continue to tolerate the abuse. But is that the best thing for her to do? To stack the legal deck in the direction of "salvaging" her marriage may mean consigning her to ten more years of abuse. Marriages where marital rape has occurred should not be saved at any cost.

Moreover, why should the criminal law be concerned with saving a marriage? This is not the province of the law. If the criminal law were in the business of promoting and saving marriages, no district attorney would ever press charges against an exhibitionist (think of his poor wife), and no judge would put a thief in jail (think of his poor children). But the criminal law, for better or worse, takes to task people who commit crimes, and the family chips fall where they may.

Historically, this has not always been the case. There was a time when, as protection of the sacrament of marriage, a wife could not testify against her husband or bring suit against him. There was also a time when a woman could not bring charges against her husband for assault, either. But both these conceptions have changed. If we are going to allow prosecution of a husband for assault despite its effects on the marriage, there is no less justification for prosecuting him for rape.

The concern with breaking up the marriage is something of a red herring. No one has any qualms about breaking up a marriage to punish a "real" rapist. The panic some people have about prosecuting a wife rapist boils down to their view of it as a crime not worth breaking up a marriage for.

In fact, if the criminal law *were* in the business of trying to break up marriages, it could find no better place to start than here. The marriage of the murderer probably deserves more solicitude than the marriage of a wife rapist. The murderer may, after all, have a happy and healthy home, which is now to be rent asunder. The wife rapist quite obviously does not.

Many people have opposed criminalizing marital rape on the grounds that it would violate the right to privacy. They have raised the imagery of the state entering people's bedrooms and private relationships and telling them what they can and cannot do. For instance, a Florida legislator said, "You know I had a chance to just look at what the Bible has to say about marriage and the Bible doesn't give the state permission anywhere in that Book for the state to be in your bedroom, and that is exactly what this bill has gone to. It's meddling in your bedroom—the State of Florida, as an entity, deciding what you can do and what you can't do."[33]

But the idea that the state does not already interfere in married people's sex lives is simply wrong. Professor William O'Donnell has pointed out the irony that whereas consensual anal intercourse in marriage is a crime (sodomy) in many states, rape is not.[34] Legislators have clearly been willing to meddle in people's bedrooms when they were sufficiently outraged.

Of course, many people object strongly to any restrictions on the private sexual activities of married couples, precisely on the grounds that they do interfere with privacy. Civil libertarians have forced the state to rescind laws that made the use of contraceptives a crime. They have also fought to defeat laws against other sexual activity, such as homosexuality and sodomy, among consenting adults. Marital rape, however, is not parallel to either consensual homosexuality or sodomy. Marital rape is by definition not a consensual act. It is not simply an offense against morals, a victimless crime; indeed, it does have a victim, a person whose liberty and autonomy are being compromised.

Rather than interfere with personal liberty, as laws against homosexuality do, a law against marital rape would actually affirm a woman's freedom of choice. It is interesting to note that the American Civil Liberties Union has departed from its usual opposition to expanding the criminal law and has taken a position in support of statutes criminalizing marital rape. As Aryeh Neier, the former executive director of the ACLU, wrote, "The law cannot be neutral on this issue. It either protects the victims of rape or it protects the rapist. If the law exempts husbands from rape charges, the implication is that it condones husbands raping wives."[35] The only privacy involved in the marital-rape exemption is the privacy of a husband to abuse his wife sexually as he pleases.

The last and most technical of the arguments offered by opponents of marital-rape law reform is to say simply that it is superfluous. Marital rape may be awful, they concede. It may be deserving of prosecution and punishment, and marital-rape victims certainly should be protected. But, they argue, all this can already be accomplished under current legal arrangements. In particular, marital-rapists can be prosecuted under assault laws; marital-rape victims can gain relief through divorce; and by suing for civil damages, marital-rape victims can exact all the retribution they want.

These legal remedies do exist. Effective to some extent, they are utilized in many of the ways these critics say they ought to be. Men who rape their wives are sometimes prosecuted for assault; women who are raped do manage to escape via divorce; and in rare cases, some victims do bring suits to recover damages from sexual assault in marriage.[36] But these solutions are inadequate in certain crucial ways. They do not afford sufficient remedies, they do not give enough protection, and, most important, they continue to sweep the problem of marital rape under the rug and treat it as no problem at all.

Assault prosecutions are a good case in point. The main problem here is that assault is not the same as rape, either inside marriage or out. If assault laws were adequate to handle the crime of rape, then we wouldn't need any rape statutes, marital or otherwise. Most rapes usually do qualify as physical assaults, too, but some do not. A woman can be coerced to have sex through a threat of economic reprisal, through a threat to harm some third party, or for some other reason. But even when physical force is used against her, the force does not necessarily reflect the full pain and humiliation of the rape. Sometimes the force seems rather minor by assault standards, in contrast to the deep and lasting psychological trauma of the rape itself.

"The existence of rape laws in general," says Marianne Stecich, "is an implicit recognition that rape laws protect against a qualitatively different sort of harm than assault and battery laws do . . . [harm to] a woman's sexual integrity and freedom of choice."[37] The insult of rape is psychological as well as physical. A woman is being coerced to have deeply intimate contact against her will. She is being degraded and stigmatized. Rape can have extremely powerful effects on a woman's ability to enjoy subsequent intimate sexual contact. This is not the same as assault. Those who say that rape can be handled by assault statutes fail to recognize the true nature and seriousness of the crime that has been committed.

Another problem with the assault-law approach to marital rape is that it postulates that rape is a different kind of crime inside of marriage, since outside of marriage, the law considers rape and assault as two qualitatively different offenses. The double standard seems to be based on the assumption that marital-rape victims don't suffer the same kind of special trauma as other rape victims, that they are somehow, in the words of William O'Donnell, "psychologically rape-proof."[38]

Unfortunately, this assumption is wrong. We hope that if our research does little else, it establishes that women who are raped in their marriages suffer long and deeply, and not just from the pain of their beatings when these occur, but also from the humiliation and violation particular to sexual offenses. In fact, the violation of intimate trust and the ongoing threat of a recurrence can make marital rape even more traumatic than stranger-rape. The special humiliation and violation of a sexual assault are present in marital rape just as in any other rape. All this suggests the wisdom and justice of considering sexual assault in marriage as the crime of rape, not just assault.

Of course, an additional reason for criminalizing marital rape under rape statutes is that rape is viewed as a more serious crime than assault; it is regarded by society with much greater horror and outrage, as reflected in the stiffer penalties handed out for the crime of rape. According to one study of federal cases, convicted rape offenders receive average sentences of 73.6 months, more than double the sentences of assault offenders, which average around 36.1 months. Convicted rape offenders are also more likely actually to end up in jail.[39]

This is not to say that convicted marital-rapists are likely to get the same sentences as other rapists, or even that penalties for a conviction under a marital-rape law would necessarily be stiffer than penalties for a conviction under a simple assault statute. But it does illustrate that rape is regarded as a far more serious crime than assault. To the extent that a sexual assault in marriage is considered a rape rather than an assault, the law will consider it a more serious crime.

All this presumably has an effect on deterrence. The horror with which a crime is regarded and the heaviness of the sentences imposed for its commission are two of the ways in which the criminal law works in theory to protect victims and deter offenders. If marital rape is treated as nothing more than an assault, the husbands are not deterred from rape to the same extent as when heavier rape penalties apply.

Thus, lumping marital rape together with assault can be criticized in four ways. (1) It fails to provide remedy for certain rape victims who are not technically assaulted; (2) it fails to give recognition to the true nature and seriousness of the offense that has been committed; (3) it fails to acknowledge that marital-rape victims, like other rape victims, suffer the particular humiliation of a sexual attack; and (4) it fails to offer an adequate and appropriate deterrent against this form of attack.

Another remedy offered up to marital-rape victims by the "alternative-remedy" proponents is to get a divorce and, if they care to, sue their husbands for civil damages. As Ralph Slovenko said, "The Divorce Court would seem a more appropriate forum than a criminal trial for the complaint of a wife who feels she cannot endure sex."[40] Of course, this is possible and often used. But the suggestion is even more vulnerable to the criticisms just leveled at the "assault" solution—it doesn't give adequate recognition of harm or provide adequate protection against the offense in the first place.

Civil actions—which are what divorce and suit for damages are—are not substitutes for criminal action. That is why we have a criminal law. After all, there is nothing to stop you from suing the thief who steals your TV or the mugger who hits you on the head. But if those were adequate remedies, we wouldn't need any criminal law.

Criminal law recognizes that violence is a crime against society as a whole, not just against the victim of the violence. It reflects a belief that some behavior is so horrible that it needs to be deterred by stronger penalties than the mere threat of suit and is so offensive that we do not leave it up to individual discretion to decide whether it will be punished. Finally, criminal law is based on the premise that certain victims who have already been wronged deserve to have the heavy burden of retributive action taken off their shoulders and assumed by society.

Marital rape is a crime that meets all of these requirements. It is serious enough to be considered a crime against society, a crime worthy of serious deterrent penalties, and a crime where the state should relieve the individual victim of the burden and responsibility of intervention. All this means that marital rape needs the backing of a criminal law, that the civil remedies of divorce and civil suit are not enough.

If we were talking about spousal homicide, there would be no such discussion of special handling. Homicide, after all, is a serious crime, the kind of crime our criminal system is set up to handle. But to many, marital rape is not viewed as sufficiently serious for the state to take the risks it must to prosecute a serious crime. Until the seriousness of marital rape is acknowledged, these arguments, however weak, will continue to be offered as adequate reasons for not treating marital rape as a crime at all.

10

Ending Marital Rape

The emphasis of this book has been on raising awareness about the seriousness of marital rape, and detailing the ways in which the problem is ignored or minimized. Once marital rape is acknowledged, the next step is to begin to mobilize to do something about it, a process that has two major steps. The first step is to reach out to the current victims to help them end the abuse and, where necessary, to extricate themselves from the relationships they are in. To do this, we need to expand self-help, social-service, and criminal-justice resources for victims. We also need to work to change the attitudes of friends, family members, and professionals, attitudes of ignorance and insensitivity that serve at present to keep marital-rape victims locked in their shame and isolation.

The second step has to focus on preventing marital rape by changing underlying social conditions that foster it. Marital rape will not be eliminated until the status of women in society is fundamentally changed. In particular, this involves the empowerment of women through improved economic, political, and social opportunities so that they are no longer the dependent and vulnerable partners in marriage. It also involves the destruction of the sexist ideology that spawns violence against women. The image of women's "proper place" and the myths about rape and women's sexuality are deeply embedded in our culture. As the general social devaluation of women declines, we believe the prevalence of marital rape will decline along with it. Unfortunately, these changes are major ones involving the very foundations of our institutions and values and will not occur easily or suddenly.

Although marital rape has been concealed and misunderstood, it shares a great deal with other, more visible problems. There are many important similarities between marital rape and wife battering, incest, and nonmarital rape. It is only in the last decade that all of these have been recognized publicly as affecting large numbers of women, and their recognition has gone through certain predictable stages, which marital rape will undoubtedly also follow.

Marital rape has, like the others, been a problem that victims have had a hard time naming, admitting, talking about, and doing something about. These obstacles can be fairly directly traced to social attitudes that have in the past minimized the problem and stigmatized its victims. A very important part of the pain provoked by such assaults comes from the isolation these victims feel. Thus, the most important priority in confronting marital rape is outreach to its victims—women who we now know are many and in pain and danger.

Intensified public information about the problem, in and of itself, has important salutary effects. Through public information, victims of marital rape can come to identify themselves and take note that others, perhaps many others, have gone through similar

187

experiences. They can feel less alone, and more justified in resisting and protesting. They can find ways to talk about their own experience with people they trust.

One important way in which outreach to victims can start is through the media. When a subject of this sort is discussed often enough on television, in the newspapers, and in popular magazines, eventually victims hear about it.

In the case of child sexual abuse, for example, this process is now well under way. Although as late as 1975 it was rarely discussed, by 1981 virtually 93 percent of the people in one survey said they had read or heard something about sexual abuse in the last year.[1] As a result, people are much better informed about the problem than they ever were. Shame about the problem is on the decline, and mental-health workers report a record number of adults and children coming forward to report such experiences and get help.[2]

This process of media exposure has begun for marital rape, but it is not nearly so advanced. In the three years before this book was written (1984), articles about marital rape had appeared for the first time in many prominent publications as well as on television. For example, *The New York Times*, *Cosmopolitan*, and *McCall's*[3] had all run feature articles on the problem. Television programs such as "Miller's Court," "Phil Donahue," and a special TV movie about the Rideout case conveyed the subject of marital rape to large national audiences. There have even been fictional portrayals of marital rape in the true-confessions magazines.

There is something real, immediate, and poignant in a victim's talking about her own experience, which can be more effective in reaching out to other victims than a hundred academic articles. In the case of incest, for example, some of the most successful publicity about the problem was done by former victims, such as Louise Armstrong, Katherine Brady, and Charlotte Vail Allen,[4] who wrote first-person accounts of their experiences and spoke on television and around the country. These courageous women made people aware of the real nature of incest.

Certainly there will be women who will perform much the same service for the cause of women raped by their husbands. Carol Coady, a marital-rape survivor who has appeared on numerous talk shows, is one such pioneer; so, too, are the women who volunteered to participate in our study; and we expect there will be many more. Through the experience of seeing them talk openly about what happened to them, other women will find the strength to open up for the first time to friends, relatives, or people they trust to give them help.

Ultimately, however, many women need outside help to deal with marital rape. Unfortunately, at the current time, this help does not exist or is inadequate. Wives who are raped, not surprisingly, need much the same kind of help as women who are battered. The problem for both groups is that many are trapped, are economically dependent, and have little leverage to use against the husbands who abuse them. As we have seen, marital rape and wife battering often go hand in hand.

The two most frequent recommendations by battered women who have "beaten" wife beating, according to a University of Wisconsin study,[5] were to contact a social-service agency or a women's group. Almost half the women mentioned one of these two resources, and their other replies made it clear that such agencies and groups offered women needed information and confidence to take some action.

Many women, however, cannot get help from agencies or women's groups because their husbands will not let them. They may live in such a reign of terror that any attempt at independence would only bring more violence down on them. These women obviously need more protection and aid than that provided by a women's group or social-service agency. For these women shelters are the only escape. They permit women to leave their homes in an emergency, without having to figure out where to stay, how to pay the rent, what to do with the children, and how to keep their husbands from harassing them. Shelters give women a kind of breathing space in which to figure out what they want to do next.

On the other hand, many women who use shelters eventually go back to their marriages. This does not necessarily mean that the shelters were a "failure": shelters may have been an effective tool for these women in ending the violence in their relationships, a very credible weapon for some women who have few other available means to stop their abuse.

The main problem with shelters is that there are not enough of them. They are expensive to run and most have had to operate on shoe-string budgets. Not very many governmental authorities have been willing to make a commitment to fund such shelters. The number of shelters for battered women multiplied rapidly across the country in the late 1970s. Whereas in 1976 there were only a half dozen, in 1980, by some estimates, there were over five hundred shelters nationwide.[6] In the early 1980s, however, under the pressure of government-funding cutbacks, the number and size of these shelters unfortunately started to decline, threatening to leave battered and raped women again without support. Appropriations from the federal government that would have helped to establish shelters failed numerous times in Congress, until 1984, when a modest appropriation for shelter activity was attached to the reauthorization act for the National Center on Child Abuse and Neglect. The federal government, however, still has no agency with a mandate to act on behalf of battered wives. The Comprehensive Employment and Training Act (CETA), which provided staff members for many shelter operations, has now been eliminated. In cities and towns where shelters have managed to continue, they are often overcrowded, yet many women in the community are unaware of their existence, especially homebound victims of marital rape. Also, the concept of a shelter is so new and unconventional in the United States that many women have a hard time imagining themselves going to one. So even where shelters exist and are known, some women still do not use them.

Another problem is that many of the shelters have not specifically reached out to victims of marital rape. Shelters in many areas are preoccupied enough with women who have been beaten, and the constituency of women who have been raped by their spouses has not, as a rule, come to their attention. Janet Geller, an early leader in the shelter movement, said in 1979, "We are just beginning to be aware that many battered wives who come in here have also been raped by their husbands. But they don't volunteer that information—we have to ask in order to learn about it."[7]

Unfortunately, many shelter workers did not routinely ask the battered women about sexual-assault experiences. In the minds of many women, this perpetuated the belief that marital rape is too shameful to talk about, even among workers who are familiar with family violence. Workers in shelters are like everybody else with respect to marital rape: they have not heard a great deal about it, and since it is a highly personal subject, both difficult and embarrassing to bring up, they have often neglected to raise it. Fortunately, however, this is changing, and some of our most valuable information about marital rape is coming from shelters.

Now that shelter workers have begun to ask women routinely about marital-rape experiences, some will undoubtedly move on to the next step: actively offering services to women raped by their husbands. They will need to start with some publicity in their communities to make contact with such women, and then try to let the women know that shelter services are available to them even if they have not been beaten.

Rape crisis centers, too, have only recently begun to orient their services toward women raped by their husbands. These are grassroots women's agencies that developed during the seventies to help women cope with the aftermath of rape. Volunteers from these agencies were trained to give support, to help women decide if and how they would report the assault, to accompany women to the police station, hospital, district attorney's office, or court, and generally to advocate on their behalf. Such agencies also provided counseling and self-help groups for rape victims.

Because wives sexually assaulted by their husbands have not defined their problem as rape, most rape crisis centers have received few calls for assistance from such victims. In 1975 a study of sixteen different rape crisis centers found that only twelve out of over three thousand calls received by the centers concerned marital rape.[8] Moreover, victims of marital rape often need a different set of services from those needed by women who are raped by strangers. They may need a place to get away from home, a restraining order, help in starting divorce proceedings. Thus, rape crisis centers will have to train their volunteers to deal with women raped by their husbands, and they will have to publicize their services in such a way that wives see the rape crisis center as an agency that deals with their particular needs.

One of the most pressing immediate needs is for self-help groups of women who have experienced marital rape. We have seen, in Chapter 7, how serious an impact marital rape can have on a woman. An important component of the trauma she suffers is her sense of isolation, shame, and self-blame. In the case of other related problems, such as child sexual abuse, self-help groups have had revolutionary effects on victims, who are greatly relieved when they learn that others have gone through much the same experience and have overcome the effects. Hearing others asserting confidently that it was not their fault, seeing others voicing their anger at their assailants, victims can very quickly come to see their own experience in a new light.

Since rape crisis centers and battered-women's shelters have sponsored self-help groups for rape victims and battered women, they are both natural agencies around which groups of marital-rape victims can coalesce. If the self-identified marital-rape victims are not numerous enough to form their own group, they can be integrated into groups of other rape victims or of battered women, with whom they undoubtedly share a great deal. But marital-rape victims have much to say to one another, and the formation of such independent groups will not only help the group members themselves, but also contribute to community consciousness raising about the problem of marital rape within the greater community.

The attitude of police and prosecutors is also a critical component in a community's response to marital rape. Where such officials take the problem seriously and assume responsibility for dealing with it, the climate for marital-rape victims can change very rapidly and dramatically. For one thing, police and prosecutors play an important role in defining societal standards. By choosing to prosecute one or two men for sexually assaulting their wives, a prosecutor can educate a whole community to the crime of forced marital rape.

Even public statements can make an important difference. When Broward County Assistant State Attorney Joel Lazarus said, "Maybe three or four years ago a woman would have said that 'being forced to have sex by (my) husband is my lot in life.' . . . Now she knows she doesn't have to take bullsh—— from anybody," it made the newspaper, and a great many Broward County residents undoubtedly got the message.[9] On the other hand, recently, when a Vermont district attorney was quoted as saying, "I don't want to get into trying rape by spouse. . . . I'm just not interested," this was also quoted in the press, giving local residents a different message.[10] In an era of changing attitudes and awareness, the pronouncements of public officials can set a tone for local opinion.

Police, too, play an important role. Many of our interviewees had strong negative preconceptions about how police would be likely to handle the report of a battering or a rape. Police departments have gained unfortunate reputations in the matter of domestic violence, and when they are known to be insensitive it puts another obstacle in the way of a woman who is contemplating getting help or getting out of an abusive situation. Among the women who had "beaten" wife beating, only a tiny 2 percent recommended contacting the police as a remedy.

In the early days of the movements concerning rape and wife beating, there was virtually a complete and universal pessimism about police departments' playing any kind of positive role in either problem. Police were viewed as being inevitably sexist and reactionary on these subjects, because police work has traditionally been so male-dominated.

However, under pressure from women's groups and enlightened legislators and criminal-justice officials, many police departments have made remarkable strides in dealing with rape and domestic violence. Some departments have established special details—often including women officers—to handle these crimes. Many have changed their protocols and procedures to be more responsive to the problems.

In police departments where special domestic-violence and sexual-assault units already exist, it will be much easier to enlist police allies in the effort to stop marital rape. One of the most important things police can do is to raise the issue routinely when answering domestic-violence calls. They should also inform women complaining of sexual assaults by their husbands that this is a crime (in states where it is) and tell them that they may file charges against their husbands. Such action will undoubtedly have a salutary effect on victims' views of their own marital-rape experiences, even if they do not press charges.

Some of the most desperately needed services are those that can treat husbands. A few such agencies have begun to develop around the country, some of the better known and most experienced being EMERGE in Boston, AMEND in Denver, and RAVEN in St. Louis. Most of these agencies provide crisis hot lines for men to call when they feel they have the urge to abuse, and they also provide self-help groups for men who want to find a way to end their violence.

The agencies have been able to claim success in ending the violence among the men they work with.[11] Unfortunately, the majority of batterers seem to have very little motivation to change or seek help, so that even the largest of these agencies rarely have more than one or two dozen active clients at any time. These clients come to the agency either because their wives have left and they have been told they have to change in order to get them back, or because they have been caught by the police and counseling has been required by the court or probation officers. Unless motivated by some such external pressure, most batterers do not seek help. In order to reach and affect the great majority of batterers, agencies like EMERGE have recognized the need to devote a substantial portion of their time and energy to public education. These efforts are designed to challenge attitudes among men that legitimize violent behavior, attitudes such as those expressed by "When I'm drinking, I can't control myself," or "Just a little slap isn't really violent." In addition to controlling the feelings that legitimize violent behavior, these men must rethink their attitudes about women and masculinity and their own need for power and control.

Unfortunately, there are not nearly enough agencies doing work of this sort. With good reason, the few funds available for domestic violence have been channeled primarily to shelters to help victims. Services to batterers have had to operate through volunteer help, shoe-string budgets, or money and effort pirated from other kinds of agencies.

The list of professionals who have the potential to help marital-rape victims is long. It includes doctors, especially family physicians, who know the patient and the family; gynecologists, who deal with women's sexual functioning; and emergency-room physicians, who treat a great number of rapes and traumatic injuries. It includes lawyers, who now handle an increasingly large volume of divorces, and marriage counselors, psychologists, and psychiatrists, who hear about and treat people's troubled relationships. It includes clergy, who, according to surveys, are the first people many Americans consult when faced with a personal problem. All these people are crucial links in providing help; yet most have not considered the problem at all.

As a first step, these professionals need to be made aware of the problem. They need to know why it occurs and how the victims react and conceal or cope with it. It is particularly urgent to dispel prejudices and misconceptions about the problem. The professional who tells a client that she really doesn't have a problem—that her husband is just a bit overenthusiastic about sex—can do a great deal of damage to a woman who is trying to cope with a painful situation.

Probably the single most important service these professionals can perform for victims of marital rape is to *ask* about it. Women who have suffered this kind of abuse often do not bring it up spontaneously. They have never heard it discussed and are ashamed and embarrassed to mention it themselves. Professionals find it an embarrassing subject, too, and often collude in the silence. By initiating discussion, professionals will give marital-rape victims the permission they need to talk about it and to get help.

When sufficiently alerted to the problem, members of various professions will undoubtedly come up with innovative approaches that are suited to the needs of women and the responsibilities of their professions. At the least, they need to know the names of referral sources, such as rape crisis centers and women's shelters. Further, they need to know how to counsel a woman to reduce her jeopardy. And they need to know about the laws in their state.

There are numerous situations in which a question about forced marital sex ought to be routine. Doctors, for example—especially gynecologists—take routine sexual histories that include questions about sexual satisfaction, history of pregnancy and contraception, and so on. A question about force in marital sexual relations would be appropriate here. Not only would the question provide the patient an opening to discuss the abuse, it also would provide information pertinent to medical treatment.

When prescribing contraceptives, medical practitioners also need to take marital rape into account. Clearly, women subject to forced sex are not good candidates for diaphragms. Doctors also need to be alerted to the possibility of forced sex in the wake of debilitating operations. They often tell women to refrain from sex without being aware that some women have little control over the situation. Doctors who advise against sex for a time after surgery

196

need routinely to ask women patients whether this is a requirement that they will have a hard time meeting. If so, doctors should
take responsibility for speaking directly to husbands. They should
also learn, if the situation warrants, to make referrals to other
professionals who can pursue the forced-sex issue further with
the women.

Lawyers, too, should be asking routine questions about sexual
and physical abuse in every initial conference with a woman seek-
ing divorce. As we indicated in Chapter 7, one of the high-risk
times for marital rape is soon after a couple separates, while a divorce document or separation agreement is in process. Lawyers
are well positioned to caution both husbands and wives about sexual assault at these times. They can alert wives to vulnerable situations—in particular, husbands coming over late at night. They
can, at the same time, warn husbands about the seriousness of
forcing their wives to have sex and the possibility of criminal prosecution and jail if they do so.

Psychiatrists, psychologists, clergy, and marriage counselors
should also consider marital rape in their assessments of individ-
uals coming to them for services. Unfortunately, though they do
usually ask about sex as a way of assessing the health of the relationship, the subject of force, either physical or sexual, rarely
comes up.

O f all the remedies proposed for helping marital-rape victims and stopping marital rape, the one that has received the most
attention is changing the law to eliminate the spousal exemption.
As we described earlier, spousal exemptions still exist in twenty-
seven states, and their effect is to deprive a woman of legal protection against a husband who sexually assaults her. Campaigns
are afoot across the country to change such exemptions.

It is important that marital rape be a crime, first, for the sake of
women who do want to prosecute. Though they may be few in
number, they are as deserving of recourse to the criminal law as

victims of any other crime. Second, we should change the law to eliminate injustice. It is important that the laws in our society reflect the value of equal protection to married women. If a law like the marital-rape exemption clashes with this important value, then the law needs to be brought into alignment. Third, the process of eliminating the spousal exemption will play an important role in raising people's awareness of the problem. Through the legislative debate and the publicity surrounding it, people will discover that marital rape is a serious and common problem that they may not have considered before.

Finally, changing the law is essential to deterrence. An important part of the marital-rape problem is that not enough husbands recognize that what they are doing is wrong, and too many wives believe that they have little right to resist and object. When a law is changed after a public debate of this sort, it will more clearly delineate where the moral boundaries are and will remind people that they can be punished if they violate these boundaries. After such a public debate and passage of a new law, it will be harder for men to believe they have a right to force their wives, and harder for a woman to feel her objections have no grounds. By raising people's consciousness about where the moral boundaries lie in our society, and threatening to punish people who violate them, a new law can presumably prevent some marital rapes that might have otherwise occurred.

It is often held that society cannot "legislate morality." However, this argument is generally applied to victimless crimes. As this study has made amply clear, rape in marriage does have victims. Society proscribes many immoral acts, such as murder and violent assault. Marital rape must be put into this category.

Prosecutions under these new laws are important for the same reason. They further extend the consciousness-raising process; they remind people about the new law; and they increase its deterrent value. People not only see legislators proclaiming marital rape as a crime; they also see men threatened with punishment—

some actually going to jail—for committing such crimes. The message is reinforced.

Realistically, however, many husband-rapists are going to rape no matter what the law says, and no matter what the courts do. We have strong laws against rape, yet rape continues. Without interventions that change basic attitudes and behavior, changing the marital-rape laws can have but a partial effect on the amount of marital rape or the plight of victims.

The prevention of marital rape requires more than legal reforms. We need to identify what kinds of social arrangements and attitudes can be changed in order to reduce the prevalence of marital rape.

The larger-scale social changes that would make the most difference for the problem of marital rape is equality for women and wives. Research consistently indicates that women are more vulnerable to abuse when they have little power and few resources. Women who are less educated, not employed outside the home, and tied down with several children to take care of are more likely to be abused.[12] These women cannot easily pick up and leave: they cannot find a place to live, bring in an income, or easily choose life alone with several dependent children. Their abusers know they can brutalize their wives because their wives have little choice but to take it.

Women are less likely to be abused if they have more power and more resources, whether in the form of money, education, or friends and family who can be counted on for support. Indeed, self-confidence is also a resource. Women with such resources on their side have alternatives to remaining in an abusive relationship; they have greater control over their lives. A husband knows he is jeopardizing his relationship by abusing such a woman, and this is one important deterrent to abuse. The women in the study on "beating wife-beating" said their most useful deterrent to abuse was the husband's fear of divorce.

It follows that social changes that result in greater equality between husbands and wives—that empower women—are likely to serve as a deterrent to marital rape. These social changes include an end to job discrimination and more educational opportunities, day-care centers to reduce the burden of child care, training programs for displaced homemakers, and laws that make child support easier to collect.

Marital rape does not exist in a vacuum. Its prevalence is closely tied to the general level of sexual aggression, and the many other kinds of sexual assault and sexual hostility that are connected to it.

The United States has one of the highest official rape rates of any Western country.[13] The exact degree of America's rape supremacy is hard to determine, since much rape, both here and in other societies, goes unreported. But the official rates are so much higher in the United States (between ten and thirty times higher than in Western Europe, for example) as to suggest that reporting differences cannot explain it all.

Recent research on rape suggests that some important ingredients of our rape-prone culture are widely shared attitudes that encourage and tolerate rape. Surveys of college student males, for example, show that a surprisingly large number admit that they would commit a rape if they thought they could get away with it.[14] These rape-prone men are more likely than other men to hold attitudes that make rape a legitimate behavior in their eyes, at least under certain circumstances.

For example, these men tend to believe that women like to be strong-armed into sex, that women who act in sexually provocative ways deserve to be raped, that women who really do not want to be raped can always resist it. Such attitudes fuel the tendency of some men to behave in sexually aggressive ways toward women, and promote sexual aggression toward their wives. These men believe that if a woman lets a man do it, she really must have wanted it. They believe that rape is a fair punishment for a woman who tries to take advantage of a man. Believing these things, they are more likely actually to commit rape on their wives.

Changing such attitudes is not easy. Beliefs and values are not rules written down somewhere that can be erased or revised. For the most part, men learn them in association with other men, particularly in adolescence, as they talk about women, about sex, about their encounters, and also through pornography. Both the peer groups and pornography give license to sexual exploitation and, further, to the idea that violence is manly. This combination is the foundation upon which physical and sexual violence against women rests.

Ending marital rape, then, is no simple goal. The steps to providing help for current victims and prosecuting the rapists alone will require enormous energy. Actually *ending* marital rape is a goal that is inseparable from the larger efforts to end the oppression of women. Physical and sexual attacks against women are not isolated events. They are part of the social fabric in which economic and legal inequalities, sexist attitudes, exploitation of women's bodies, and violence are all interwoven.

It is important to understand marital rape as part of this social fabric. By hearing the testimony of women who have survived rape in marriage and by helping to break the silence surrounding this problem, we can begin to rescind the license to rape.

Appendix A:

The Research Study

THE SURVEY

Our findings on the prevalence of marital rape were obtained as part of a larger survey about the problem of child sexual abuse. We had hired a survey research organization (The Center for Survey Research at the University of Massachusetts) to interview six hundred parents of children age six to fourteen in the Boston metropolitan area. (For more details on the survey, see David Finkelhor, *Child Sexual Abuse: New Theory and Research* [New York: Free Press, 1984].) Since the subject matter already dealt with sexual victimization and we had a corps of highly trained and sensitive interviewers, the survey was easily adapted by adding questions about marital rape.

One part of the interview was in the form of a self-administered questionnaire. This contained some of the more sensitive questions in the study, including whether the respondent had ever been sexually victimized as a child. To this self-administered portion of the interview, we added a question about sexual assault in marriage and cohabiting relations. They were phrased as follows: "Has your spouse ever used physical force or threat to try to have sex with you? 1. Yes 2. No."

The question was limited to "physical force or threat" in accordance with our decision to focus only on this kind of coercion. We used the word "try" so as not to exclude unsuccessful assaults. The questionnaire was administered to 323 women in the spring of 1981, a sample that was scientifically selected through an area-probability methodology as being representative of the Boston population, but with one limitation: it is only representative of Boston-area women who had a child between the ages of six and fourteen living with them. We imposed this condition on the survey because we obviously needed women who had children in the appropriate age range, since the primary focus was on the sexual abuse of children. As a result, the survey contains:

- no women who were married but did not have children;
- no women who were married but whose children were old enough to have left home;
- very few women who had been married less than six years.

A breakdown of the results follows, in Tables A-1 through A-10.

TABLES

A "p" (probability) of less than .05 gives social scientists
confidence that the results are statistically significant,
that is, that they represent real differences between groups
rather than accidental or random findings.

TABLE A-1   SEX BY PHYSICAL FORCE OR THREAT
BY TYPE OF ASSAILANT

Assailant	*% Reporting* *(N = 326)*
Stranger	3
Someone you knew a little	3
Friend	3
Date	10
Relative	1
Spouse (or cohabiting partner)	10

$p < .01$

TABLE A-2   RATES OF FORCED SEX IN MARRIAGE
BY CURRENT MARITAL STATUS

Status	*% Reporting* *Forced Sex*	*N*
Married	3	224
Separated/divorced	25	76
Cohabiting	20	5
Cohabiting now separated	23	13
Widowed	14	7

$p < .001$

TABLE A-3   RATES OF FORCED SEX IN MARRIAGE
             BY EDUCATIONAL LEVEL

Education	% Reporting Forced Sex	N
Did not complete H.S.	16	43
H.S.	9	141
College or more	8	139

p<.10

TABLE A-4   RATES OF FORCED SEX IN MARRIAGE BY
             EDUCATIONAL LEVEL, CONTROLLING FOR
             MARITAL STATUS

Marital Status and Education	% Reporting Forced Sex	N
Married/cohabiting		
Did not complete H.S.	12*	17
H.S. or above	3*	212
Separated/divorced/widowed		
Did not complete H.S.	19	27
H.S. or above	26	69

*p<.05

TABLE A-5   RATES OF FORCED SEX IN MARRIAGE
             BY CURRENT FAMILY INCOME

Income	% Reporting Forced Sex	N
Less than $10,000	24	67
$10–24,999	10	111
$25–34,999	5	56
More than $35,000	2	67

p<.001

TABLE A-6   RATES OF FORCED SEX IN MARRIAGE
             BY RACE

Race	% Reporting Forced Sex	N
White	10	287
Black	5	20

$p = $ N.S.

TABLE A-7   RATES OF FORCED SEX IN MARRIAGE
             BY RELIGION

Religion	% Reporting Forced Sex	N
Protestant	16	92
Catholic	6	181
Jewish	3	29
No religion	18	22

$p < .01$

TABLE A-8   RATES OF FORCED SEX IN MARRIAGE
             BY CURRENT AGE

Current Age	% Reporting Forced Sex	N
Under 30	18	48
31–35	10	89
36–40	6	87
41–45	4	53
46–50	9	34
Over 50	21	14

$p < .10$

TABLE A-9   RATES OF FORCED SEX IN MARRIAGE
BY BACKGROUND OF SEXUAL VICTIMIZATION
AS A CHILD

Background	% Reporting Forced Sex	N
Sexually victimized as a child	22	49
Not sexually victimized as a child	7	275

$p<.001$

TABLE A-10   RATES OF FORCED SEX IN MARRIAGE
BY CURRENT EMPLOYMENT STATUS

Employment Status	% Reporting Forced Sex	N
Homemaker	7	108
Employed	9	198
Unemployed/disabled/student	33	18

$p<.01$

THE INTERVIEWS

In-depth interviews with fifty women who had been sexually assaulted by their husbands made up the second part of our study. These were not the same women as in the Boston survey. Family-planning agencies were our main source of interviewees (56 percent). Other sources included self-referrals (26 percent), referrals via battered-women's shelters (16 percent), and respondents to an ad in *Ms.* magazine (10 percent).

Each volunteer was interviewed for one to two and a half hours, usually at the agency where she had been recruited, or, in the case of the *Ms.* recruits, over the phone. Kersti Yllo conducted most of the interviews, although David Finkelhor spoke with several, who said they had no qualms about talking to a man. The interviews were loosely structured conversations in which we asked about a wide variety of matters: what the woman's childhood had been like, how she had met her husband or partner, how the relationship had progressed, how much violence there had been, and so forth. All the interviews were tape-recorded, but we promised the interviewees that in anything we wrote we would disguise their stories so that no one would be able to identify them or anyone else. We kept no record of the names of the women we interviewed. Most women indicated little apprehension either about the interview or the tape recorder, and opened up easily once the interview got going.

Aside from some transient awkwardness in giving details about the sexual assault itself, the majority of the women talked freely and even eagerly about their experiences. At the end each interviewee was paid ten dollars for her time, and told about resources that were available locally should she be interested in counseling, women's groups, shelters, or attorneys. Several of the interviewees felt so positive about the research that they either refused to take the money or insisted that it be donated to the agency where we were doing the interviewing.

The women came from a wide variety of social classes and family situations. One of our interviewees was a college professor; several were nurses; several were teachers; others were social workers. Over a third had college educations. We also interviewed a share of women who had never worked outside the home, some who had worked in factories or as secretaries, and even one who called herself an "exotic" dancer.

The participants were all white, however. Although there were many ethnic groups represented—Italian, French, English, Scandinavian, Polish—there were no blacks or Hispanics. In large part, this reflects the racial composition of the part of New England where almost all the research was conducted. It is unfortunate that our research does not encompass the experience of minority women, and we hope that the need for such a perspective will soon be filled.

The age range of the women we interviewed was wide. Some of them were under twenty and told of experiences they had undergone just months earlier. Others were well into middle age and talked about incidents that had occurred ten and twenty years before. The median age of the group was thirty-two; one-third were under twenty-five and one-sixth were over forty.

The relationships our interviewees described took in the full spectrum. Some had been married just a short time. One woman who had been married just three months left her husband after he raped her twice. On the other hand, several women had been in marriages that lasted twenty to twenty-five years, long stints in which they had been continually subjected to violence and sexual abuse. The median length of relationships was six years; a quarter were less than two years long, another quarter more than ten.

A quarter of the women were not officially married at all, but were cohabiting. We had evidence from our Boston survey that cohabitors are at particularly high risk of being sexually assaulted by their partners. We included cohabitors in the study as long as they had set up a joint household with their partners. Much of the agony of a marital sexual assault has to do with being raped by the person one loves, with whom one lives.

It is true that in the strictly legal view of rape, cohabitors are somewhat different from married couples. The "raping license" primarily applies to husbands, although in some states the spousal exemption has been extended to cohabitors as well. However, the division between cohabiting and marrying is becoming increasingly blurred among young people today. But, more important from a psychological point of view, being sexually assaulted by a cohabitor is very much the same as being assaulted by a husband.

Although the sample was diverse in many respects, there was one unexpected similarity in the group: all but three of the women were either divorced or separated from the men who raped them.

We wish that this could be taken to mean that over 90 percent of the women who are sexually assaulted by their husbands eventually leave them. Unfortunately, we know from our Boston survey that this is not the case. Although divorced and separated women have experienced a disproportionate share of forced sex, a large number of women who are raped by their husbands do not leave them. And some, as we know from our interviews, do not leave them for a long, long time. So we are forced to conclude that women who are raped and continue to live with their husbands just did not volunteer for the interviews. Some of them no doubt were afraid that their husbands might find out and punish them for it. Others, we guess, were not yet sure whether they wanted to leave or take some other action. Participating in the study might have required the acknowledgment of a problem they were not yet ready to deal with.

Unfortunately, the fact that we talked to few women who were still living with their rapist-husbands builds a troubling bias into our report. Our study is essentially about sexual assaults that occur in marriages that eventually come to an end, about sexual assaults seen through the eyes of divorced and separated wives. Other kinds of marital rape may be different, and we may be missing some important information on them as a result. We will know whether this is the case when we do further research, talking— we hope—to more wives who are still living with their husbands.

A statistical breakdown of the women we interviewed follows, in Tables A-11 through A-30.

TABLES

TABLE A-11   SOURCE OF INTERVIEWEES

Source	% (N = 50)
Family-planning agencies	46
Shelters	16
Self-referrals	28
Ad	10

TABLE A-12   AGE OF RESPONDENTS AT TIME OF INTERVIEW

Age	% (N = 50)
Under 20	2
21–25	30
26–30	12
31–35	24
36–40	16
41–45	6
46–50	6
51 +	4

TABLE A-13   EDUCATIONAL BACKGROUND
              OF RESPONDENTS

Level	% (N = 44)
Some H.S.	14
H.S. degree	16
Some college	30
College degree	29
Graduate degree	11

Median education = 13.7 years

TABLE A-14   CURRENT EMPLOYMENT STATUS
              OF INTERVIEWEES

Status	% (N = 50)
Professional	14
Business/managerial	2
Clerical/sales	20
Skilled worker	4
Unskilled worker	32
Not employed outside home	22
Student	6

TABLE A-15   VIOLENCE IN BACKGROUND
              OF INTERVIEWEES

Type	% (N = 46)
Physical abuse	24
Sexual abuse	41
Violence between parents	25

TABLE A-16   TYPE OF RELATIONSHIP WITH
              ASSAILANT

Type	% (N = 50)
Married	76
Cohabiting	24

TABLE A-17   LENGTH OF RELATIONSHIP

Years	% (N = 48)
Less than 1 year	4
1–5 years	41
6–10 years	30
11–15 years	15
15+ years	10

Median Length = 6.0

TABLE A-18   CURRENT RELATIONSHIP
              BETWEEN INTERVIEWEE
              AND ASSAILANT

Status	% (N = 50)
Divorced	52
Separated	24
Ended (unspecified)	18
Still living together	6

TABLE A-19   MAJOR AREAS OF CONFLICT
WITH SPOUSE

Conflict	% Reporting This Conflict (N = 41)
Money	29
Drinking	27
Sex	49
Children	27
Jealousy	27
Housework	5
Jobs	17

TABLE A-20   HOW OFTEN FORCED SEX
OCCURRED

Frequency	% (N = 46)
Once only	28
Twice	11
3–10 times	7
11–20 times	4
More than 20	50

TABLE A-21   DURING WHAT PARTS OF
RELATIONSHIP INTERVIEWEE
REPORTED FORCED SEX

Period	% Reporting Forced Sex in That Period (N = 42)
Early in relationship	31
Middle	40
End	69
After separation or divorce	24

TABLE A-22   CHARACTERISTICS OF MARITAL-
RAPE EXPERIENCE

Characteristics	% *(N = 50)*
Did partner ever	
Force sex after beating	40
Force vaginal intercourse	94
Force anal intercourse	32
Force oral-genital sex	20
Force sex in presence of others	24

TABLE A-23   WHERE FORCED SEX
OCCURRED

Place	*% Reporting* *(N = 42)*
Bedroom	74
Living room	14
Outside home	12

TABLE A-24   INFLUENCE OF ALCOHOL ON
FORCED SEX

	% *(N = 46)*
Husband drinking during at least one episode	70
Husband not drinking during any episode	30

TABLE A-25   DID INTERVIEWEE EVER
              SUCCESSFULLY RESIST
              PARTNER'S FORCED SEX?

	% (N = 44)
Yes	27
No	73

TABLE A-26   REPORTED ENJOYING FORCE ON
              AT LEAST ONE OCCASION

	% (N = 42)
Enjoyment on at least one occasion	12
Never any enjoyment	88

TABLE A-27   DID INTERVIEWEE TELL
              ANYONE ABOUT FORCED SEX?

	% (N = 48)
Told	60
Did not tell	40

TABLE A-28   INTERVIEWEE'S DEFINITION OF THE EXPERIENCE

	% (N = 46)
Called it rape	72
Did not call it rape	28

TABLE A-29   TYPE OF MARITAL RAPE ACCORDING TO AUTHORS' CLASSIFICATION

Type of Marital Rape	% (N = 50)
Battering rape	48
Force-only rape	40
Obsessive	6
Mixed	6

TABLE A-30   VICTIMS OF BATTERING AND
                FORCE-ONLY RAPES COMPARED

Characteristic	Battering (N = 24)	Force-Only (N = 20)
Average age	29	33
Business/professional job	5%	46%*
Years of education	12.9	15.1
Physically abused as child	38%	6%*
Sexually abused as child	44%	47%
Weight of partner (pounds)	176	200*
Length of relationship (years)	5.2	8.1†
Violence in relationship	100%	78%*
Violence before sex	57%	17%‡
Forced anal sex	35%	15%†
Forced oral sex	26%	10%
Successful resistance	19%	39%†
Partner drinking in episode	82%	61%†
Told anyone	63%	61%
Raped more than 20 times	50%	22%*
Raped after separation	29%	20%
Regarded episode as rape	67%	74%

* p<.05
† p<.01
‡ p<.001

Appendix B:
The California Experience

In the debate over removing the spousal exemption to rape, much concern has been expressed over how or even whether a revised law would work. Opponents of the change have raised several different specters of insidious consequences that would ensue if marital rape is criminalized. For example, they have warned that deleting the spousal exemption would risk flooding the criminal-justice system with frivolous complaints brought by "vindictive" wives. They have also raised the fear that cases brought under such a law would be impossible to prosecute, either because wives would be unreliable witnesses or because the cases would boil down to her word against his. In short, they have predicted that marital-assault prosecutions would bog down and frustrate the criminal-justice system.

Until recently, arguments over these claims have been mostly hypothetical, since there has been little empirical evidence against which to judge them. However, now that several states have eliminated the spousal exemption and have gained experience about what happens once the exemption is removed, it is possible to see how a spousal-rape law works in actuality.

A state well situated for a study of the effects of criminalizing marital rape is California. California changed its law as early as January 1980, and has had a total of more than four years' experience without the spousal exemption. As the most populous state in the country, California has also generated a large number and variety of spousal-rape cases. Moreover, since the change of the law was hotly debated and widely publicized in California, public attention to marital-rape cases has been relatively high there, making information on the subject easier to collect.

On the other hand, using California to study the operation of marital-rape prosecutions has some drawbacks. California's legal situation with regard to marital rape is not entirely parallel to that of other states that have criminalized rape between husband and wife who are still living together. When California changed the law on spousal rape, the legislators did not merely delete the spousal exemption. Instead, they drafted a totally new section of the criminal code on the matter of spousal rape. One important special condition attached to the California spousal-rape law is that victims were required (until recently) to bring such charges within thirty days of their occurrence. Another is that marital rape, unlike nonmarital rape, can be a misdemeanor rather than a felony. Nonetheless, a great deal of valuable insight into the question of whether marital rape is a viable legal concept can be gleaned by looking at the situation in California.

Gathering the needed data on the operation of the marital-rape law in California has not been a simple task. Unfortunately, the state Bureau of Criminal Statistics does not keep very thorough or very detailed information on marital-rape prosecutions, even though an important public-policy issue is at stake.[1]

So the staff of the National Clearinghouse on Marital Rape (NCMR) has been forced to compile data on its own—a frustrating and cumbersome task. Marital-rape cases have been identified in a variety of ways, but primarily through a newspaper clipping service. The staff of the Clearinghouse, after hearing about a marital-rape prosecution, made contacts with the journalists, attorneys, prosecutors, court officials, and sometimes rape crisis workers familiar with the case, in an effort to get as much detail as possible about the events of the case, the backgrounds of the offender and the victim, and the disposition of the case within the legal system. District attorneys were generally the best and most reliable sources of information. Occasionally, these officials referred NCMR staff to other cases that had not been identified through the news clipping service.

Altogether, NCMR staff identified forty-two cases of marital rape that came to the attention of the police or courts from January 1980 through December 1981. Though this is not necessarily a complete inventory of all such cases, one piece of evidence suggests that it is at least fairly thorough. The state Bureau of Criminal Statistics did compile what it believed to be a complete tally of all arrests for marital rape in 1980. This official tally showed eleven arrests. For the comparable time period, the NCMR inventory showed seventeen cases that even the official reporting statistics did not pick up.

Nonetheless, it must be said that although NCMR believes its inventory to be fairly complete, there is no way of knowing how totally complete it is. Moreover, without such information, we cannot vouch for the inventory's representativeness, either. There is every reason to believe that the cases not identified, if there were any, would be less sensational cases that did not proceed as far in the criminal-justice system. In other words, the cases that were identified would be more brutal, contain more evidence, and be more likely to result in a hearing or a trial that would bring it to greater public attention than other cases. Whether this group of cases is thus biased, we do not know.

The first thing to note about the cases compiled by the NCMR is that they were, on the whole, extremely brutal. The cases include one in which a woman was raped with a crowbar and a sixteen-inch tire iron and then had her breasts slashed with the same instruments. In another, a woman complained that her husband forced her to have sex with other men and dogs. In still another, the fugitive husband murdered the victim before he could be apprehended for her rape. The use of knives and guns was a common feature among these cases, and several included very severe beatings.

A second important feature of the cases was that a majority of the rapes occurred between spouses who were separated, sometimes very recently so. In only 18 percent of the cases were the couples still living together. It is not surprising that cohabiting couples constitute a minority of cases. Wives who are still living with their husbands no doubt have a much more difficult time seeing what happened to them as a rape and choosing to present such charges to the police. Also, a woman who is living in a separate household would expect less skepticism and ridicule on the part of police when she made such a charge. And it may be easier for such women to establish evidence of force and nonconsent. As time goes on, normative standards change, and women become more aware of their rights, then the proportion of cases involving cohabiting spouses may increase.

Nonetheless, the inventory does clearly establish that prosecution of cases in which the husband is still living with his wife is possible, and can result in convictions. Removing the exemption for cohabiting spouses also has a "multiplier" effect, we suspect, on the prosecution of estranged husbands, because it engenders a great deal of publicity about the problem. Prosecutors, police officers, and women in general learn about the possibility of charging spouses with rape. This no doubt leads to an increased number of cases involving estranged husbands as well as cohabiting husbands.

The NCMR researchers were able to gather some valuable information about the offenders as well as about the court disposition (see Table B-1). The offenders were, by and large, young.

TABLE B-1   SOCIAL CHARACTERISTICS OF
OFFENDERS ON CASES OF
SPOUSAL RAPE BROUGHT TO
PUBLIC ATTENTION, 1980–81
IN CALIFORNIA

Characteristics	*% Cases* *(N = 39)*
Marital situation at time of rape	
Living together	18
Separated	82
Age	
Under 25	33
26–30	31
Over 30	33
Not ascertained	2
Race	
White	59
Black	18
Hispanic	18
Not ascertained	5
Occupation	
Blue-collar	31
White-collar	13
Unemployed	31
Not ascertained	26

Sixty-four percent were under thirty, and 33 percent under twenty-five. This corresponds to what we found in our interview population: marital rape, at least as it comes to public attention, is predominantly a younger man's crime.

Occupationally, the offenders whose marital rapes came to public attention were also a lower-status group. Large numbers—31 percent—were unemployed, and another 31 percent were blue-collar workers. This may not tell us anything about marital rape in general, however. We have to remember that it is typically men from lower social classes who are the clientele of the criminal-justice system; well-to-do criminals tend to be more successful at evading detection and prosecution. Nonetheless, this inventory of cases shows that some middle-class marital-rapists are being prosecuted. The law is being applied to a spectrum of husbands, not just one class.

The racial and ethnic breakdown of the offenders shows a distribution roughly typical of the California population as a whole. Of those whose race we could ascertain, about two-thirds were white and the remaining third divided between black and Hispanic.

The most interesting information we can glean from these cases is not so much about the phenomenon of marital rape itself but, rather, about how the phenomenon is handled in the criminal-justice system. The cases are certainly not a representative set of marital rapes, the vast majority of which we know are never reported. But they are in all likelihood a representative sample of cases that make their way into the legal system. What happens to marital-rape cases once they arrive there? (Table B-2 contains a breakdown on outcomes.)

First of all, a substantial number of cases get dropped before they go very far—often before trial, and sometimes before arraignment. In 28 percent of the cases in this sample, the charges were dropped. Unfortunately, the information on why this happened is not among the most reliable. Many times the reason given depends on the perspective of the person giving it. District attorneys often choose to drop charges because they think they do not have a good case, but then blame it on lack of cooperation by the wife; the wife may see the dropping of charges as the district attorney's decision. The real state of affairs is difficult to determine.

It is certain that in some cases charges are dropped at the request of the wife. Where NCMR researchers could ascertain the reasons the wife gave for such requests, they included such things as (1) the wife was pressured by relatives of the offender to drop the charge, (2) the wife did not want to face the embarrassment of a trial, (3) the wife forgave her husband and wanted him

TABLE B-2   DISPOSITION OF CASES OF
MARITAL RAPE BROUGHT TO
POLICE ATTENTION 1980-81
IN CALIFORNIA

Disposition	% Cases (N = 39)
Charge dropped	28
Cases prosecuted	72
Outcomes:	
Plea of guilty to spousal rape	31
Plea of guilty to other charge(s) only	13
Guilty verdict to spousal rape—jury	10
Guilty verdict to spousal rape—nonjury	2
Guilty verdict to other offense—jury	8
Not guilty—jury	5
Not guilty—nonjury	2
Total guilty	64
Sentences	
Probation, suspended, fine	26
Jail less than 2 years	15
Jail more than 2 years	23

back, or (4) the wife got what she most wanted (divorce and protection) in other ways.

Of course, another common reason, especially in wife-abuse cases, is fear of further retaliation by the husband.

It does not appear from the available information that the cases where the charges were dropped were frivolous or fraudulent. Some of these dropped charges involved severe assaults, replete with injuries and witnesses. In fact, one case involved the woman who had been raped and battered with the tire iron.

The remaining cases (72 percent) went on for prosecution, and of these a remarkable 89 percent (twenty-five out of twenty-eight) resulted in a conviction. There were several routes to a conviction. The most common was a simple guilty plea on the part of the offender: 60 percent (seventeen of twenty-eight) of the offenders pleaded guilty, usually to the charge of spousal rape itself. In a little less than a third of such pleas, though, the charge was bargained down to another charge, usually assault or battery.

In eleven cases the offender pleaded not guilty and went to trial. Of these, eight resulted in a guilty verdict—seven by a jury and one by a judge. There were three not-guilty verdicts handed down to marital-rape charges, two by a jury and one by a judge. (Actually in the one jury acquittal, there were two jury trials: one ended in a deadlock, the other in an acquittal.)

In all twenty-five cases that resulted in a guilty finding, the offenders received sentences of some sort. Most of the sentences, however, were not particularly severe. Ten of the convicted men received no jail term whatsoever. Most of these got off with suspended sentences and fines. Some were remanded to counseling and one was ordered to do community service.

Fourteen of the twenty-five did go to jail or prison, though, with sentences ranging from thirty days to sixteen years. The severe sentences tended to be meted out only when other crimes had been committed as well. In the case where a sixteen-year sentence was imposed (by a judge), the offender had abducted and raped another, unrelated woman during the same episode in which the spousal rape had occurred. A man who held his son hostage with a sawed-off shotgun was sentenced to four years. The longest sentence meted out for a marital rape uncomplicated by other crimes and weapon violations was three years, though the maximum possible term for felony spousal rape is eight years.

From an analysis of these thirty-nine cases, it is possible to draw some important conclusions about how the criminal-justice system deals with the issue of marital rape once it is criminalized. These conclusions contribute directly to the debate on policy that has been taking place in legislatures and courts for the last few years.

First, there is little evidence that the courts will be swamped by a large number of marital-rape complaints. Thirty, forty, or even fifty cases reaching the courts over a two-year period in a state of twenty million people is a minuscule burden on the system. In the case of California, the load works out, as far as we can tell, to be approximately one case per year per million inhabitants. At that rate, most states in the country can probably expect fewer than a dozen prosecutions a year following the criminalization of spousal rape. If we are talking about states where the exemption still exists but applies only to a husband and wife who live together, the increase in the number of cases will be even smaller.

As to whether these cases will be frivolous, the opposite would appear to be true. If California's experience holds true elsewhere, the cases that will come to court will tend to be the most blatant, the most brutal, and the most heinous.

Of course, these conclusions only apply to cases in the courts. Those opposed to criminalizing marital rape are also concerned about the police's being inundated with a large number of unfounded complaints. From the data we have collected, we cannot draw any conclusions about the experience of the police.

Clearly, a large number of marital-rape charges are later dropped. As in the case of wife abuse, where similarly large numbers of cases are dropped, there is controversy about why the attrition rate is so high. Police and prosecutors tend to blame the wives for being fickle. Advocates for battered women tend to blame the criminal-justice system for being insensitive.

The key problem, however, lies not in determining who is to blame but in improving the level of mutual cooperation between victims and the criminal-justice system. Where special victim-assistance programs have been set up around the country, for example, and where prosecutors have learned more about the dilemmas facing victims, this level of cooperation has increased.[2]

If the cases noted here are any indication, women do not drop charges because they were trumped up in the first place. Rather, they retract charges after having suffered from fear, embarrassment, or pressure by relatives. Sometimes sensitive and ongoing personal contact between the prosecutor and the victim is enough to prevent case attrition. As prosecutors recognize marital rape as a legitimate crime and gain more experience with marital-rape cases, we expect that they will learn how best to work with victims to ensure their participation, and their record will improve.

Perhaps the most impressive finding from our analysis of the California experience is that, contrary to what many opponents have claimed, marital-rape prosecutions can be very effective indeed. The number of convictions as a percentage of the number of cases brought in California was actually extraordinarily high. A conviction was obtained in 64 percent of all cases where a charge was lodged, in fully 89 percent of all cases that reached the prosecution stage.

Compare this, for example, to nonmarital-rape prosecutions. According to statistics for 1980 gathered by the California State Department of Justice, of 3,126 cases of forcible rape where arrests were made, 1,368 or 44 percent resulted in a conviction. Of all forcible-rape cases reaching actual prosecution (2,026), the percentage resulting in conviction was 67 percent.[3] In short, the prosecution of marital-rape cases in California was more likely to result in success than the prosecution of nonmarital rape.

This is an extremely important finding, since a main concern of prosecutors is that their time will be wasted in pursuing marital-rape cases. It is often imagined that the prosecution of such cases will be hampered by lack of evidence, doubt about whether sex was forced or consensual, and prejudice among jurors against the idea of convicting a husband on the word of his wife. The experience in California does not bear out these concerns. Marital-rape cases, once they get to the stage of prosecution, do not seem to be extraordinarily time-consuming. In three-fifths of the cases, the offenders pleaded guilty, avoiding the necessity of a trial altogether. Hence the system actually worked very efficiently from a prosecutor's point of view.

It is significant that so many offenders pleaded guilty to the spousal-rape charge. Defendants and their attorneys did not automatically think that it was an easy charge to beat. Nor did prosecutors; otherwise, they might have been more likely to bargain away the spousal-rape charge. Thus the charge can be an effective piece of ammunition for the prosecutor.

The number of guilty pleas meant that there were rather few jury trials involving marital-rape charges, making it harder to tell from the California experience how juries react to marital rape. However, there was a small amount of evidence. Of the nine jury trials, seven ended in convictions, showing that juries are not averse to bringing in a conviction against a husband, as some might have thought. Moreover, the fact that there were at least two acquittals may relieve others of the fear that no man will ever receive a fair hearing in front of a jury on such a charge—a difficult position for us to believe, given the amount of popular skepticism that exists about marital rape.

The California statistics speak quite favorably to the criminalization of marital rape in other states. The law worked as many thought it would, and perhaps even better than expected. It resulted in a modest number of prosecutions of particularly outrageous cases. The conviction rate among those prosecuted was remarkably high, higher than comparable rates for nonmarital rape prosecutions. The marital-rape charge held up in the plea-bargaining process as well as in jury trials. The outcome of the California experience should give encouragement to other jurisdictions that are considering whether to allow the prosecutions of husbands who rape their wives.

Notes

1
LICENSE TO RAPE

1. *Illinois Annotated Statutes*, ch. 38, 11-1 (1977).
2. Matthew Hale, *History of the Pleas of the Crown*, vol. I. 1680 (Emlyn ed., 1847).
3. Dennis Drucker, "The Common Law Does Not Support a Marital Exception for Forcible Rape," *Women's Rights Law Reporter* 5 (1979):181–200.
4. Susan Brownmiller, *Against Our Will: Men, Women and Rape* (New York: Bantam, 1975).
5. Del Martin, *Battered Wives* (New York: Pocket Books, 1976).
6. New Jersey v. Smith, 85 N.J. 193 (1981); Commonwealth of Massachusetts v. Chretien, Mass. Adv. Sh. (1981) 661, 417 N.E.2d 1203 (Mass. 1981); Florida v. Smith, 401 So. 2d 1126 (5th D.C.A. 1981), retr. denied July 30, 1981; People v. Liberta, N.Y. Court of Appeals (December 1984).
7. Mari Jo Buhle and Paul Buhle, *The Concise History of Woman Suffrage* (Champaign: University of Illinois, 1978).

8. Ruth Barnes Moynihan, "Abigail Scott Duniway's Advice to Women on Sex and Health," paper delivered to the Fifth Berkshire Conference of Women Historians, July 1981.
9. Theresa Hughes, quoted in Linda Gordon, *Woman's Body, Woman's Right* (New York: Grossman, 1976).
10. Quoted in ibid.
11. Quoted in Buhle and Buhle, *Concise History.*
12. Gordon, *Woman's Body.*
13. We used a number of techniques to increase the opportunity for candor in the interviews. All our interviews were conducted by interviewers from an experienced survey research organization. All were given training in how to develop rapport with interviewees on this delicate subject. Our questions about forced sex in marriage were preceded by a long conversation in which many other kinds of sexual matters, including childhood sexual victimization, were discussed extensively.

   The question on forced sex in marriage was located in a special self-administered section of the questionnaire, so that interviewees did not have to reveal their marital-rape experience to the interviewer at all. After privately marking the answer on the questionnaire, they placed it in a sealed envelope and gave it to the interviewer.
14. Diana Russell, *Rape in Marriage* (New York: Macmillan, 1982).
15. Russell did not ask these women outright whether they had been raped. Surveys that have asked women that question have generally obtained much lower figures for marital rape, because women who are assaulted by their husbands do not often think of themselves as rape victims. Instead Russell asked her interviewees, "Did you ever have any kind of unwanted sexual experience with your husband(s)?" If the respondent said yes, the interviewer asked her to describe the experience briefly. It was on the basis of that description that

Russell decided whether the experience fitted the legal definition of rape.

16. Russell, *Rape in Marriage*.

2

THE MYTH AND REALITY OF MARITAL RAPE

1. There are a number of estimates available in the literature of the percentage of battered wives who also report marital rape: 36 percent of a sample of 304 battered women in ten shelters in Minnesota (Peggy Spektor, "Testimony Before the Law Enforcement Subcommittee of the Minnesota House of Representatives," February 29, 1980); 36 percent of a sample of battered wives at a shelter in Portland, Maine (Jean Giles-Sims, *Wife-Beating: A Systems Approach* [New York: Guilford, 1983]); 37 percent of 325 battered women from a number of shelters (Mildred Daley Pagelow, "Double Victimization of the Battered Woman: Victimized by Spouses and the Legal System," paper presented at the American Society of Criminology, San Francisco, 1980); 32 percent of a sample of forty women responding to an ad in *Ms.* magazine asking about marital violence (S. Prescott and C. Letko, "Battered Women: A Social-Psychological Perspective," in *Battered Wives*, ed. Maria Roy [New York: Van Nostrand, 1977]); 46 percent of a sample of eighty-two St. Louis wives whose husbands had assaulted them (Nancy Shields and Christine Hanneke, "Battered Wives' Reactions to Marital Rape," paper presented to the National Research Conference on Family Violence, Durham, N.H., 1981); 35 percent of the randomly selected eighty-seven marital-rape victims in Diana Russell's study reported violence ranging from hitting, kicking, or slapping to beating and slugging (Diana Russell,

Rape in Marriage [New York: Macmillan, 1982]); 59 percent of 403 self-identified battered women interviewed by the Battered Women's Research Project in Denver (Roberta Thyfault, "Sexual Abuse on the Battering Relationship," paper presented to the Rocky Mountain Psychological Association, Tucson, 1980); 34 percent of a self-identified group of battered women in Pittsburgh said they had been "raped," and 43 percent said they had been "forced" (Irene Frieze, "Causes and Consequences on Marital Rape," paper presented at the American Psychological Association, Montreal, 1980). The clustering between 33 and 50 percent is quite conspicuous in these samples, which were done at different times, in different places, using different questions.

2. Reports on the frequency of marital rape available in the literature run as follows: Frieze, "Causes and Consequences": 59 percent of marital-rape victims were raped more than once; Russell, *Rape in Marriage*: 31 percent said it occurred only once, 71 percent said it occurred more than once, and 34 percent said it occurred twenty times or more; Pagelow, "Double Victimization": 74 percent said it occurred more than once; Thyfault, "Sexual Abuse": 83 percent of marital-rape victims had been assaulted more than once; Shields and Hanneke, "Reactions": 87 percent were raped more than "once or twice," and 37 percent were raped "many times" or "all the time."

3. Frieze, "Causes and Consequences."

4. Russell, *Rape in Marriage*.

5. Shields and Hanneke, "Reactions"; Frieze, "Causes and Consequences."

6. Norman Mailer illustrates this point in his short story "Time of Her Time," where the protagonist uses anal intercourse to retaliate against a woman he feels has derogated his masculinity (Norman Mailer, *Advertisements for Myself* [New

York: Plenum, 1959]; see commentary in Kate Millett, *Sexual Politics* [New York: Ballantine, 1970].

3
THREE TYPES OF MARITAL RAPE

1. Diana Russell, *Rape in Marriage* (New York: Macmillan, 1982), p. 101.
2. Some writers use the term "battered wife" to apply to any woman who has been hit. Our terminology reserves "battered" and "battering" for relationships where the violence is chronic, like those described by Lenore Walker in *The Battered Woman* (New York: Harper and Row, 1979). We do not mean to imply, however, that a single violent episode in a marriage is of minor importance. On the contrary, we believe that such an episode can have devastating and permanent consequences for a woman.
3. Nicholas Groth, *Men Who Rape* (New York: Plenum, 1979).
4. Ibid., pp. 13–14.
5. Ibid., p. 25.
6. Ibid., pp. 30–31.
7. Ibid., p. 44.

4
MEN WHO RAPE THEIR WIVES

1. Brian G. Gilmanton, "Swinging: Who Gets Involved and How?," in *Marriage and Alternatives*, ed. Roger Libby and Robert Whitehurst (Glenview, Ill.: Scott, Foresman, 1977).
2. Nicholas Groth, *Men Who Rape* (New York: Plenum, 1979).
3. Shere Hite, *The Hite Report on Male Sexuality* (New York: Alfred A. Knopf, 1981).

5
MARITAL RAPE AND MARITAL SEXUALITY

1. Shere Hite, *The Hite Report on Female Sexuality* (New York: Alfred A. Knopf, 1976).
2. Suzanne Brogger, *Deliver Us from Love* (New York: Delacorte, 1976).
3. Hite, *Female Sexuality.*
4. Alfred C. Kinsey et al., *Sexual Behavior in the Human Female* (Philadelphia: Saunders, 1954), cites the following references on the traditional Catholic position of marital duty: H. Davis, *Moral and Pastoral Theology in Four Volumes*, vol. 4 (New York: Sheed and Ward, 1947); P. C. M. Kelly, *The Catholic Book of Marriage* (New York: Farrar, Straus and Young, 1951). According to Professor William D'Antonio of the University of Connecticut, the contemporary American church no longer actively holds the traditional position, however.
5. Ralph Slovenko, "Rape of a Wife by Her Husband," *Medical Aspects of Human Sexuality*, July 1974, pp. 65–66.
6. George Levinger, "Systematic Distortion in Spouses' Reports of Preferred and Actual Sexual Behavior," *Sociometry* 29 (1966): 291–99.
7. Morton Hunt, *Sexual Behavior in the 1970's* (New York: Dell, 1974).
8. Levinger, "Spouses' Reports."
9. Hunt, *Sexual Behavior.*
10. Charles Westoff and Norman B. Ryder, *The Contraceptive Revolution* (Princeton: Princeton University Press, 1977).
11. Irene Frieze, "Causes and Consequences of Marital Rape," paper presented to the American Psychological Association, Montreal, 1980.
12. Nicholas Groth, *Men Who Rape* (New York: Plenum, 1979).

13. Eugene Kanin, "An Examination of Sexual Aggression as a Response to Sexual Frustration," *Journal of Marriage and the Family* 12 (1967): 428–33.
14. Dorothy Dinnerstein, *The Mermaid and the Minotaur: Sexual Arrangements and the Human Malaise* (New York: Harper and Row, 1976).
15. John Gagnon and William Simon, *Sexual Conduct: The Social Sources of Human Sexuality* (Chicago: Aldine, 1973); John Gagnon, *Human Sexualities* (Glenview, Ill.: Scott, Foresman, 1977).
16. Alan Gross, "The Male Role and Heterosexual Behavior," *Journal of Social Issues* 34 (1978): 87–107.
17. Bernie Zilbergeld, *Male Sexuality* (New York: Bantam, 1975).
18. Ibid.
19. Gagnon, *Human Sexualities*.
20. Constantina Safilios-Rothschild, *Love, Sex and Sex Roles* (Englewood Cliffs, N.J.: Prentice-Hall, 1977).

6
RESISTING MARITAL RAPE

1. M. Joan McDermott, *Rape Victimization in 26 American Cities* (Washington, D.C.: U.S. Department of Justice, 1979).
2. Pauline Bart, "Avoiding Rape," final report on NIMH Grant MH-12931, University of Illinois, Chicago, 1979.
3. Ibid.
4. In a seemingly growing number of cases, however, abused wives are turning to violent defense. We have only recently begun to recognize that many women who kill their husbands do so after years of physical (and probably sexual) abuse at their hands (Angela Browne, "Assault and Homicide at Home: When Battered Women Kill," [in *Advances in Ap-*

plied Social Psychology 3 (1984): 000–000]; Ann Jones, *Women Who Kill* [New York: Holt, Rinehart and Winston, 1980]; Faith McNulty, *The Burning Bed* [New York: Harcourt Brace Jovanovich, 1980]).

5. Jean Giles-Sims, *Wife Battering: A Systems Theory Approach* (New York: Guilford, 1983).

6. Murray A. Straus, "A Sociological Perspective on the Prevention and Treatment of Wife Beating," in *Battered Women*, ed. Maria Roy (New York: Van Nostrand, 1977).

7. Lee H. Bowker, *Beating Wife-Beating* (Lexington, Mass.: Lexington Books, 1983).

8. Ibid, p. 124.

9. In a fascinating study, two social psychologists showed men and women vignettes of rape episodes, in some of which the victim resisted and some not. Men tended to see the resistance in very positive terms, as evidence of intelligence on the part of the victims. Women, however, saw the resistance as a less intelligent response (Judith Krulewitz and Janet Nash, "Effects of Rape Victim Resistance, Assault Outcome and Sex of Observer on Attributions About Rape," *Journal of Personality* 47 [1979]: 557–74).

10. Diana Russell, *Rape in Marriage* (New York: Macmillan, 1982).

11. Irene Frieze, "Causes and Consequences of Marital Rape," paper presented to the American Psychological Association, Montreal, 1980.

7

THE IMPACT OF MARITAL RAPE

1. Irene Frieze, "Causes and Consequences of Marital Rape," paper presented to the American Psychological Association, Montreal, 1980.

2. Helene Deutsch, *The Psychology of Women* (New York: Grune and Stratton, 1944); Sigmund Freud, "The Economic Problem of Masochism," in *Collected Papers,* vol. 2 (London: Hogarth Press, 1948).

3. Julia R. Schwendinger and Herman Schwendinger, "Rape Myths: In Legal, Theoretical and Everyday Practice," *Crime and Social Justice* 1 (1974): 18–26.

4. Ann Burgess, "Physical Sexual Misconduct and Patients' Responses," *American Journal of Psychiatry* 138 (1981): 1335–42.

5. Nicholas Groth, *Men Who Rape* (New York: Plenum, 1979).

6. David Finkelhor, *Sexually Victimized Children* (New York: Free Press, 1979).

7. Robert Hillman, "Psychopathology of Being Held Hostage," *American Journal of Psychiatry* 138, no. 9 (1981): 1193–97.

8. John Gagnon, *Human Sexualities* (Glenview, Ill.: Scott, Foresman, 1977).

9. Warren Gadpaille, *Cycles of Sex* (New York: Scribner's, 1975).

10. Nancy Shields and Christine Hanneke, "Battered Wives' Reactions to Marital Rape," paper presented to the National Research Conference on Family Violence, Durham, N.H., 1981.

11. Quoted in Mark Christenson, "The Honeymooners," *Oui Magazine,* September 1980, pp. 77–80.

12. Lloyd Shearer, "Rape in Marriage," *Parade Special,* April 22, 1979.

13. Senator Jeremiah Denton, Talking Points for Presentation at U.S. Senate Judiciary Committee Hearing, November 18, 1981.

14. Diana Russell, *Rape in Marriage* (New York: Macmillan, 1982).

15. Pauline Bart, "Rape Doesn't End with a Kiss," *Viva* 2 (1975): 39–42, 100–101.

8

MARITAL RAPE AND THE LAW: STATE STATUTES AND PUBLIC OPINION

1. Joanne Schulman, "The Marital Rape Exemption in the Criminal Law," *Clearinghouse Review* 14, no. 6 (1980): 538–40; Joanne Schulman, "Marital Rape Exemption Chart," mimeo, National Center on Women and Family Law (copies available at $1.50 each from the Center at Room 402, 799 Broadway, New York, N.Y. 10003).

2. The fact that no marital-rape charges have been brought in three of these states suggests that district attorneys believe that an exemption is in force.

3. William O'Donnell, "Consensual Marital Sodomy and Marital Rape—The Role of the Law and the Role of the Victim," paper presented at the annual meeting of the Academy of Criminal Justice Sciences, 1980.

4. When a matter is not specifically dealt with by an American statute, the English common law is said to apply. "Common law" refers to the Anglo-American legal tradition as it was in 1776, when the United States became independent.

5. Dennis Drucker, "The Common Law Does Not Support a Marital Exception for Forcible Rape," *Women's Rights Law Reporter* 5 (1979): 181–200.

6. B. A. Babcock, A. E. Freedman, E. H. Norton, and S. C. Ross, *Sex Discrimination and the Law* (Boston: Little, Brown, 1975).

7. Drucker, "Common Law."

8. New Jersey v. Smith, 85 N.J. 193 (1981).

9. Commonwealth of Massachusetts v. Chretien, Mass. Adv. Sh. (1981) 661, 417 N.E. 2d 1203 (Mass. 1981).

10. N.J.S.A. 2C:14-5(b).

11. According to accounts of debate in the legislature at the time

the bill passed, legislators originally imposed a thirty-day limitation, in part to satisfy the concerns of some legislators that women might bring belated charges of marital rape in order to qualify for state funding of abortions under the state provision that allows funding for abortions resulting from rape (Laura X, personal communication).

12. Joanne Schulman, personal communication.
13. Schulman, "Marital Rape Exemption."
14. Generally, the "voluntary-social-companion" exemption serves not to eliminate the charge altogether, but to lessen the degree of the charge and thus the penalty (see Schulman, "Marital Rape Exemption Chart").
15. Charles Jeffords, "Attitudes of Texas Residents Towards Criminal Sanctions Against Forced Marital Sex," Ph.D. dissertation, Sam Houston State University, 1981.
16. Peter Rossi, Emily Waite, Christine Bose, and Richard Berk, "The Seriousness of Crimes: Normative Structures and Individual Differences," *American Sociological Review* 39 (1974): 224–37.
17. Joyce E. Williams and Karen A. Holmes, *The Second Assault: Rape and Public Attitudes* (Westport, Conn.: Greenwood Press, 1981).
18. Charles Jeffords and Thomas Dull, "Demographic Variations in Attitudes Toward Marital Rape Immunity," unpublished mimeo, Sam Houston State University, Huntsville, Texas, 1979.
19. "Residents Questioned in Marital Rape Poll," *West Hartford Connecticut News,* July 6, 1981.
20. Ibid.
21. Jeffords and Dull, "Demographic Variations."
22. Williams and Holmes, *Second Assault.*
23. Jeffords and Dull, "Demographic Variations."
24. Jeffords, "Attitudes."
25. Ibid.

26. Susan and David Klemmack, "The Social Definition of Rape," in *Sexual Assault,* ed. Marcia Walker and Stanley Brodsky (Lexington, Mass.: Lexington Books, 1976).
27. Williams and Holmes, *Second Assault.*
28. Marvin Wolfgang and Marc Riedel, "Race, Rape and the Death Penalty," in *Forcible Rape: The Crime, the Victim and the Offender,* ed. Duncan Chappell, Robley Geis, and Gilbert Geis (New York: Columbia University Press, 1977).

9

THE DEBATE OVER CRIMINALIZING MARITAL RAPE

1. Matthew Hale, *History of the Pleas of the Crown,* vol. 1, 1680 (Emlyn ed., 1847).
2. Gilbert Geis, "Lord Hale, Witches and Rape," *British Journal of Law and Society* 5 (1978): 284.
3. Moira Griffin, "In 44 States, It's Legal to Rape Your Wife," *Student Lawyer* 9 (1980): 21–23, 58–61.
4. Martin Schwartz, "The Spousal Exemption for Criminal Rape Prosecution," *Vermont Law Review* 7, no. 1 (1982): 33–57.
5. Regina v. Clarence, 22 Q. B. D. 23 (1888).
6. Ernst Livneh, "On Rape and the Sanctity of Matrimony," *Israel Law Review* 2, no. 3 (1967): 415–22.
7. "Note: The Marital Rape Exemption," *New York University Law Review* 52 (1977): 306–23.
8. Joanne Schulman, personal communication, 1982.
9. Quoted in Dennis Drucker, "The Common Law Does Not Support a Marital Exception for Forcible Rape," *Women's Rights Law Reporter* 5 (1979): 181–200.
10. B. A. Babcock, A. E. Freedman, E. H. Norton, and S. C. Ross, *Sex Discrimination and the Law* (Boston: Little Brown, 1975).
11. "Note: The Marital Rape Exemption."

12. Quoted in Dick Polman, "Subject to Change—Sexual Assault in the Home: Is Marriage a License to Rape?," *Hartford Advocate,* February 18, 1981.
13. M. Field and H. Field, "Marital Violence and the Criminal Process: Neither Justice nor Peace," *Social Service Review* 47 (1973): 121–40.
14. Carol Bohmer, "Judicial Attitudes Toward Rape Victims," in *Forcible Rape: The Crime, the Victim and the Offender,* ed. Duncan Chappell, Robley Geis, and Gilbert Geis (New York: Columbia University Press, 1977).
15. Gilbert Geis, "Rape in Marriage: Law and Law Reform in England, U.S., Sweden," *Adelaide Law Review* 6 (1979): 284–303.
16. This short history of the Rideout case comes from the following sources: Laura X, "The Rideout Trial," mimeo, National Clearinghouse on Marital Rape, Berkeley ($1.00 per copy); Michele Celarier, "I Kept Thinking I Could Help Him," *In These Times,* January 10–16, 1979.
17. *San Francisco Examiner Chronicle,* December 24, 1979.
18. Peter Sandrock, "Letter to Honorable Richard Tulisano, Chairman of the Judiciary Committee of the Connecticut State Legislature," February 24, 1981.
19. Peter Sandrock, "Letter to Women's History Research Center," July 7, 1980.
20. Sandrock, "Letter to Tulisano."
21. Renee Binder, "Why Women Don't Report Sexual Assault," *Journal of Clinical Psychiatry* 42 (1981): 437–38.
22. Moira Griffin, "In 44 States."
23. Ibid.
24. Bohmer, "Judicial Attitudes."
25. Charles Burt quoted in Mark Christenson, "The Honeymooners," *Oui Magazine,* September 1980, pp. 77–80.
26. Binder, "Why Women Don't Report"; Diana Russell, *Sexual Exploitation: Rape, Sexual Abuse and Sexual Harassment* (Beverly Hills: Sage, 1984).

27. Donal MacNamara and Edward Sagarin, *Sex, Crime and the Law* (New York: Free Press, 1977).

28. Sandrock, "Letter to Research Center." Besides the Rideout case, the other three cases were: State v. Larry Allen Fox (Benton County) convicted April 1980; State v. Danny Clarno (Curry County) convicted March 1980; State v. Carol Franklin West (Clatsop County) convicted April 1979.

29. "Husband Is Jailed for Assaulting His Wife," *Peninsula Times Tribune* (Palo Alto, California), May 5, 1980.

30. Mary Katherine Daugherty, "The Crime of Incest Against the Minor Child and the Statutory Responses," *Journal of Family Law* 17, no. 1 (1978–79): 93–115.

31. Ralph Slovenko, "Rape of a Wife by Her Husband," *Medical Aspects of Human Sexuality,* July 1974, pp. 55–66.

32. Quoted in Duncan Chappell and Peter Sallmann, "Rape in Marriage Legislation in South Australia: Anatomy of a Reform," unpublished article, 1981.

33. Quoted in floor debate on HB 680 (bill to criminalize marital rape), May 29, 1980.

34. William J. O'Donnell, "Consensual Marital Sodomy and Marital Rape—The Role of the Law and the Role of the Victim," paper presented at the annual meeting of the Academy of Criminal Justice Sciences, 1980.

35. Aryeh Neier quoted in Griffin, "In 44 States."

36. John South, "Wife's Sizzling $2 Million Suit Against 'CHiPs' Star," *National Enquirer,* October 7, 1980.

37. "Note: The Marital Rape Exemption."

38. O'Donnell, "Marital Sodomy and Marital Rape."

39. Data for the year ending June 30, 1979, from Annual Report of the Director of the Administrative Office of the United States Court, reprinted in *Sourcebook of Criminal Justice Statistics 1980,* ed. Michael Hindelang et al. (Washington: U.S. Department of Justice, 1981).

40. Slovenko, "Rape of a Wife."

10
ENDING MARITAL RAPE

1. David Finkelhor, *Child Sexual Abuse: New Theory and Research* (New York: Free Press, 1984).
2. Ibid.
3. J. C. Barden, "Confronting the Moral and Legal Issue of Marital Rape," *New York Times,* June 1, 1981; Richard Amdur, "Conjugal Rape," *Cosmopolitan,* February 1981, p. 108; Martha Hewson, "Outlawing Marital Rape," *McCall's,* October 1981, p. 48.
4. Louise Armstrong, *Kiss Daddy Goodnight* (New York: Hawthorne, 1978); Katherine Brady, *Father's Days* (New York: Seaview, 1979); Charlotte Vail Allen, *Daddy's Girl* (New York: Wyndham Books, 1980).
5. Lee H. Bowker, *Beating Wife-Beating* (Lexington, Mass.: Lexington Books, 1983).
6. Debra Kalmuss and Murray A. Straus, "Feminist, Political, and Economic Determinants of Wife Abuse Services in American States," in *The Dark Side of Families: Current Family Violence Research,* ed. David Finkelhor, Richard Geller, Gerald Hotaling, and Murray Straus (Beverly Hills: Sage, 1983).
7. Quoted in Morton Hunt, "Legal Rape," *Family Circle,* January 9, 1979.
8. Richard Gelles, "Power, Sex and Violence: The Case of Marital Rape," in *Family Violence* (Beverly Hills: Sage, 1979).
9. Rosanne Ginter, "Legal Decisions Open Way for Rape Charge by Spouse," *Hollywood* [Florida] *Sun-Tattler,* October 12, 1981.
10. Elizabeth Slater, "Group Wants Marital Rape Included in Assault Laws," Vermont Press Bureau, October 27, 1981.
11. David Adams and Isidore Penn, "Men in Groups: The Social-

ization and Resocialization of Men Who Batter," paper presented to the American Orthopsychiatric Association, New York, 1981. (For more information on EMERGE, write Room 206, 25 Huntington Avenue, Boston, Mass. 02116.)

12. Irene Frieze, "Causes and Consequences of Marital Rape," paper presented to the American Psychological Association, Montreal, 1980.

13. Gilbert Geis, "Forcible Rape: An Introduction," in *Forcible Rape: The Crime, the Victim and the Offender,* ed. Duncan Chappell, Robley Geis, and Gilbert Geis (New York: Columbia University Press, 1977).

14. Neal Malamuth, "Rape Proclivity Among Males," *Journal of Social Issues* 37 (1982): 138–57.

APPENDIX B: THE CALIFORNIA EXPERIENCE

1. Conversation with Charlotte Rhea, California Bureau of Criminal Statistics, February 8, 1982.

2. Terry Fromson, "The Prosecutor's Responsibility in Spouse Abuse Cases," in *The Victim Advocate* (Chicago: National District Attorneys Association, 1978).

3. Adult Felony Arrest Dispositions, State of California Department of Justice, Sacramento, 1981. For figures showing even lower success rates for rape prosecutions in other localities, see Thomas McCahill, Linda Mayer, and Arthur Fischman, *The Aftermath of Rape* (Lexington, Mass.: Lexington Books, 1979).

Index

249